The SAGE CommText Series

Editor:
F. GERALD KLINE
Director, School of Journalism and Mass Communication
University of Minnesota

Associate Editor:
SUSAN H. EVANS
Department of Communication, University of Michigan

This new series of communication textbooks is designed to provide a modular approach to teaching in this rapidly changing area. The explosion of concepts, methodologies, levels of analysis, and philosophical perspectives has put heavy demands on teaching undergraduates and graduates alike; it is our intent to choose the most solidly argued of these to make them available for students and teachers. The addition of new titles in the CommText series as well as the presentation of new and diverse authors will be a continuing effort on our part to reflect change in this scholarly area.

—F.G.K. and S.H.E.

Michael E. Roloff

INTERPERSONAL COMMUNICATION
The Social Exchange Approach

Volume 6. The Sage COMMTEXT Series

SAGE PUBLICATIONS   Beverly Hills   London

This book is dedicated to three people: my wife, Karen, and my daughter, Erika, who give me great joy, and my grandmother, Trella Swain Roloff (1901-1980), who gave me love and support for which I am eternally grateful.

For information address:

SAGE Publications, Inc.
275 South Beverly Drive
Beverly Hills, California 90212

SAGE Publications Ltd
28 Banner Street
London EC1Y 8QE, England

Printed in the United States of America

Library of Congress Cataloging in Publication Data

Roloff, Michael E.
   Interpersonal communication.

   (The Sage commtext series ; v. 6)
   Bibliography: p.
   1. Social exchange. 2. Interpersonal communica-
tion. I. Title. II. Series: Sage commtext
series ; v. 6.
HM132.R653   302.2   81-4451
ISBN 0-8039-1604-3   AACR2
ISBN 0-8039-1605-1 (pbk.)

SECOND PRINTING, 1982

CONTENTS

ACKNOWLEDGMENTS

Throughout the completion of any project, an individual incurs obligations to many people. An author writing about the Social Exchange Theories would be doubly remiss in not attempting to discharge some of these obligations through publicly expressed gratitude. While I was a graduate student at Michigan State University, Professors Santo Camilleri and Donald Cushman provided me with my initial introduction and critique of these theories. Professor Gerald R. Miller suggested important applications of social exchange in interpersonal communication, and Professor Bradley S. Greenberg assisted me greatly in my research on interpersonal conflict. While at the University of Kentucky, Professor Robert Bostrom gave me the opportunity to express my thoughts about social exchange to my colleagues at the Southern Speech Communication Convention. Ms. Jill Reiner was very instrumental in the preparation and presentation of those ideas in that forum. Recently, Professor Charles Berger assisted me in the search for current literature and served as a sounding board for applications of the Social Exchange Theories. Ms. Carol Mikkelsen provided able assistance in typing the manuscript. Ms. Toni Roloff spent considerable resources finding obscure citations. Professor Susan Evans's comments about the initial draft were thorough and useful. Finally, Karen Roloff provided her usual able assistance in the preparation of revisions.

AUTHOR'S PREFACE

During my academic career, I have often been asked to teach courses which provide a general survey of theories of communication. Typically, the graduate and undergraduate students who take such courses are seeking a general introduction to the content areas which communication scholars study. As relative newcomers to the discipline, I have found their reactions to be quite interesting.

These students tend to have two general comments about the field. First, they are amazed and sometimes dismayed by the breadth of the phenomena studied by communication scholars. One can certainly sympathize with the student who faces theories focusing on cognitive processes related to persuasion at the beginning of the course and, by the end, has studied interpersonal relationships, small groups, organizations, and the mass media. Their amazement is often compounded when they become aware of the variety of empirical and humanistic methods used to study this diverse content. Nonetheless, most students leave these courses impressed with the richness of the field.

A second, somewhat negative reaction stems from the theoretical borrowing in which we have engaged. Even a cursory examination of the major subdivisions in communication reveals a large number of theories developed by scholars from other disciplines. In persuasion, social psychological theories such as Cognitive Dissonance Theory, Social Judgment Approach, and Expectancy Value Theory are typically discussed. Small group communication draws heavily from the study of group dynamics in social psychology. The study of organizational communication is often guided by Systems Theory. Mass communication effects have been studied using psychological theories such as Social Learning Theory and sociological perspectives such as diffusion of innovation. While many students are pleased when they discover new applications of theories they have studied in other classes, some do complain of redundancy. Indeed, one can be sympathetic given the saturation of theories such as Cognitive Dissonance Theory into classes ranging from persuasion to mass communication.

However, duplication notwithstanding, our discipline has benefited from theoretical perspectives developed by scholars outside our field. Communication is a young discipline and has gained important insights from research conducted in older disciplines. In addition, the dissemination of theories across disciplines will, it is hoped, move the social sciences toward a more integrated approach to human behavior rather than a restricted and segmented one. In any case, "academic chauvinism" does not seem to be a productive way to explore any phenomenon.

It is, however, the case that too much borrowing can be dangerous. We may at times be tempted to inappropriately apply a theory to communication which was developed for other forms of behavior. In such cases, we may be prompting one of two opposite effects: distorting the logic of the theory to fit communication, or distorting communication to fit the logic of the theory.

Because of the potential for knowledge expansion from examining theories both within and without, and the concomitant dangers of distortion arising from the inappropriate use of these theories, it would seem important that we study in detail the assumptions of a theory before we make wholesale use of it. The purpose of this book is to study a set of theories that have loosely been labeled Social Exchange Theories. These theories are often treated as a single theory despite the fact that they find their origins in different disciplines (sociology, psychology and social psychology). Furthermore, their assumptions about human behavior are different.

Many current explanations of interpersonal communication hint at, but never explicitly draw links between, their thinking and one or more of these theories. Miller and Steinberg (1975), for example, assume that the purpose of communication is environmental control. People communicate with others in order to achieve a variety of desired outcomes including financial, physical, or social rewards. Knapp (1978) has noted that understanding why we choose to pursue, maintain, or end relationships may be enhanced by examining the potential rewards and costs associated with a relationship. Finally, Wilmot (1979) has suggested that dyadic relationships develop based upon what individuals are willing to do with and for each other.

In each case, the authors are pointing to an important influence on our interpersonal communication: people tend to engage in certain communication behaviors with certain people, in certain situations which advance their own self-interest. This assumption does not mean that people always seek to exploit one another, but that people prefer environments and relationships that provide desirable outcomes. Certainly, the self-interest of both individuals can be met providing a mutually satisfying experience rather than an exploitative relationship. An ideal relationship would seem to be one in which two individuals are able to provide one another with sufficient benefits so that the relationship is a dependable source of satisfaction for both. Indeed, McCall and Simmons (1978) argue that reward dependability is a major bond that ties two people together into a relationship.

The assumption that a motivating force in interpersonal communication is self-interest is consistent with the Social Exchange Theories. However, the various Social Exchange Theories differ in other content areas, and it is necessary that we explore these differences. The differences may provide us with important insights into the interpersonal communication process.

In order to fully explore the potential of the Social Exchange Theories, this book will seek to answer three questions: (1) What are the various Social Exchange Theories and how do their assumptions differ? (2) How do the various Social Exchange Theories view a variety of interpersonal communication phenomena, e.g., relational development, self-disclosure, interpersonal conflict and conflict resolution? and (3) What are the strengths and weaknesses that arise from using the Social Exchange Theories to analyze interpersonal communication?

To answer these questions, five chapters have been developed. Chapter 1 will focus on definitions of processes involved in social exchange and interpersonal communication. Included in this chapter will be a discussion of terms such as social exchange, self-interest, and interpersonal communication. Chapter 2 will provide a discussion of five Social Exchange Theories: Homans' (1961, 1974) Operant Psychology Approach, Blau's (1964a) Economic Exchange Model, Thibaut and Kelley's (1959, 1978) Theory of Interdependence, Foa and Foa's (1974) Resource Theory, and Walster, Berscheid, and Walster's (1976) Equity Theory. Chapter 3 will focus on how these five theories would apply to interpersonal attraction, relational development, and self-disclosure. Since all five theories do not specifically address all of these issues, extensions will be made consistent with the theoretical position. Chapter 4 describes how these five theories would analyze interpersonal conflict and how conflicts might be resolved. The final chapter will examine the strengths and weaknesses of using these theories to examine interpersonal communication.

Before moving onward, a final objective of this book should be noted. When this author was an undergraduate, certain types of books and courses were devalued. To describe a course or text as taking a "cookbook approach" was tantamount to accusing it of being conceptually vacuous and, therefore, useless. At that time, a course which presented or advanced theories was extremely valued. After becoming a professor, I discovered that the word "theory" changed from having positive connotations to being a term associated with the conceptually vacuous. Since this book is aimed at both professionals and novices, I hope that all groups will again see the value and richness of a theory. Theories are the ideas by which we might come to understand phenomena around us and, it is hoped, create positive change in our environments.

Michael E. Roloff

Evanston, Illinois

1

SOCIAL EXCHANGE
Key Concepts

In order to understand how social exchange and interpersonal communication are related, we examine the key processes that characterize them. This chapter explores social exchange concepts such as resources, rewards, costs, and self-interest. It also describes current thinking about interpersonal communication. Finally, interpersonal communication is reconceptualized as a social exchange phenomenon.

What men call friendship is only a reciprocal conciliation of interests, an exchange of good offices; it is in short simply a form of barter from which self-love expects to gain something.

Francois, Duc De La
Rochefoucauld
1678

It would seem that the sentiments expressed by this seventeenth century French author would be very foreign to twentieth century Americans. Just as we have progressed dramatically in almost all aspects of human endeavor over the past three centuries, interpersonal relationships have also changed. To assume that people form their relationships based on self-interest, not unlike the mechanism suggested by Adam Smith as the guiding force in economics, would be a sad commentary on interpersonal communication. After all, twentieth century Americans are told: "It is better to give than receive." "Give until it hurts." "Give so that others may prosper." "Forgive and forget."

While these popular adages may represent ideals, even a casual reflection about the state of interpersonal relationships in our society would suggest that the ideals are not often realized. The number of marriages ending in divorce is increasing. Even people who have attempted to avoid the restrictions of marriage have begun using the courts as arbiters of their disputes, and some people are beginning to develop marriage contracts to insure equity in their relationships. Indeed, this author is aware of a couple who agreed upon their divorce settlement prior to their marriage! An interpersonal cynic might be prompted to state: "Love means never having to say you're sorry because apologies are never enough."

While this author is not going to defend the argument that people involved in interpersonal relationships are necessarily engaged in mutual exploitation, we will examine a set of theories that argue that the guiding force of interpersonal relationships is the advancement of both parties' self-interest. The theories do not assume that self-interest is bad, but instead suggest that the recognition of self-interest will actually enhance a relationship. These theories are generally categorized as Social Exchange Theories. To understand them, it is necessary that we understand the terminology involved. The discussion of these key concepts is organized into three divisions: social exchange processes, interpersonal communication, and interpersonal communication as social exchange.

SOCIAL EXCHANGE PROCESSES

In this section, we will examine the various concepts used to describe social exchange. Three key questions will be addressed: (1) What is social exchange? (2) What is exchanged? and (3) Why do we engage in social exchange?

What is Social Exchange?

At first glance, the notion of an exchange seems like a relatively simple idea. Generally, an exchange can be thought of as a transference of something from one entity to another in return for something else. Foa and Foa (1974, 1976) have suggested that an exchange unit involves a proaction and a reaction. A person gives or denies a resource to another (proaction) which elicits a certain response from the other person (reaction).

Emerson (1969: 1972a, b, 1976) has noted that some exchanges can be thought of as involving a single person relating to environment. For example, a child may repeatedly go into the kitchen to play in the cupboards, which may often result in finding boxes of cookies. This view of exchange is very much similar to that of learning in operant psychology. The exchange of rewards with the environment prompts the repetition of behavior. However, Emerson also notes that other exchanges involve two people relating to one another. Instead of an active person relating to a relatively passive environment, this second form of exchange involves two active persons each constituting the other's major environmental cue. For example, a child may come to learn that the "magic word" *please* is a necessary but not sufficient condition to receive cookies from mother. The child has learned a condition which will cause a significant environmental cue (mother) to provide something enjoyable (cookies). The mother has learned that providing the child with a cookie prompts a socially desirable behavior: gratitude. The two behaviors are interdependent.

Of the two forms of exchange described by Emerson, the second form seems to have the most utility for interpersonal communication scholars. We generally define interpersonal communication as a symbolic interaction between people rather than between a person and an inanimate environmental cue. However, even the recognition that social exchange involves two people masks its inherent complexity.

A variety of exchanges may take place between two people. At least two gross categories might be recognized: economic and social. Blau (1964a) has suggested several differences between the two. First, economic exchange involves specific obligations between two people, whereas social exchange involves unspecified obligations. When a person enters into a business contract, it is typically the case that the obligations incurred by both parties are clearly (at least to the lawyers) spelled out. When two people enter into a social exchange, they typically do not specify the form of exchange. When I help put up my neighbor's storm windows, I do not specify an obligation to help me with mine. One or both of us may feel an obligation has been incurred, but we have not agreed as to how it might be met.

Second, economic exchange involves specified time frames in which an obligation is to be repaid. Social exchange leaves the time period unspecified. My neighbor may not repay the debt to me this winter, but seek to repay it in the spring when I need to take my storm windows down.

Third, while the objects of economic exchange are open to bargaining, the objects of social exchange usually are not. For example, I have often heard both male and female undergraduates complain about traditional dating behavior. Both groups seem aware that an unstated obligation imposed by our culture is that the male provides the female with certain tangible rewards (e.g., a meal, movie, or flowers) and the female becomes obligated to return attention and, in some cases, affection. These obligations seem to be understood by both parties (even though they may choose to reject them). Indeed, open negotiation might well change the nature of the relationship and perhaps threaten its continuation.

Fourth, economic exchanges are based upon belief in the legal system, whereas social exchange is based upon trust. As stated earlier, economic exchange is generally guided by a contractual obligation that is enforced by the legal system. However, when two people engage in social exchange they must trust the good will of the other to prompt a reciprocal exchange. If no response is forthcoming, the person is often left with denial of future exchanges as an only recourse.

Fifth, economic exchanges tend to be impersonal, whereas social exchanges create feelings of personal obligation, gratitude, and trust. Since two businesspeople are protected in their dealings by the law, no special trust is required for their exchange, nor is any special trust necessarily created. Obligations are met not because of any special feeling for one another, but because of a myriad of formal sanctions which are available. Since social exchange lacks formal sanctions, it is much easier to attribute positive or negative feelings to the exchange person. As such, Blau argues that social exchange is often the impetus for the development of interpersonal relationships.

Sixth, the rate of exchange in economics is well defined, whereas the rate of exchange in social situations is not. We can find out from day to day the worth (or lack of same) of the American dollar in regard to other currencies or precious metals. Furthermore, this value can be related to a variety of goods. However, social exchange of objects is often difficult to describe in terms of relative value. How much is one compliment worth in terms of gratitude, loyalty, or other compliments? Indeed, we often have to resort to economic standards to determine the equity of our social exchanges. One student, after hearing a lecture about social exchange, turned to another and said: "You rat! I invited you to my house for steaks and you invited me to your house for hotdogs!!!"

Seventh, the value of economic benefits is easily detached from the individual who provides them, whereas social benefits often gain or lose value depending upon who gives them. The value of a dollar remains the same regardless of the bank from which you received it. However, the value of a compliment might increase or decrease depending upon who pays it.

While Blau's distinctions are useful, there are limitations to his analysis. There may be significant variations even within the types of exchange he

identifies. Blau suggests that economic exchanges tend to be more impersonal than social exchanges. While this may be true in most cases, we all
have encountered businesspeople who have developed feelings of trust and
gratitude for business associates through the process of buying and selling
to each other. In addition, not all exchanges in relationships remain as
unspecified or nonnegotiable as Blau suggests. We noted earlier that some
people are finding relational contracts to be quite useful as a means of
maintaining or restoring equity to their relationships. Indeed, some have
argued that such devices can be used as a form of therapy for troubled
marriages (Stuart, 1969; Weiss, 1975). In sum, not all economic or social
exchanges are the same.

In addition, the distinctions between economic and social relationships
are not sufficiently clear so as to make them mutually exclusive. McCall
(1970) has argued that people attempt to keep their task-oriented interactions (encounters) separate from their attempts to validate their self-
concepts (relationships). As such, boundary rules in task-oriented encounters attempt to screen out certain roles which the interactants might find
disruptive for completion. On the other hand, boundary rules in relationships seek to control the types of activities and alternative relationships in
which the partners are involved. Therefore, a business axiom might be
"Leave your personal problems at home when you come to work," and a
familial rule might state "Don't discuss business at the dinner table."
However, an examination of our society leads to the conclusion that the
distinctions between relationships and encounters are no longer clear.
Dual-career marriages may result in both spouses working for the same
organization. Their organizational concerns become intertwined with their
familial interests. High interest rates on home mortgages have forced many
young marrieds to borrow money from their parents, in addition to banks,
for the purchases of their homes. Suddenly, familial relationships take on a
decidedly economic characteristic as decisions about interest rate and
repayment schedules are discussed by family members. Indeed, paying off
the loan with interest may not be sufficient repayment of the social
obligation incurred when borrowing money from one's family. The family
may expect greater signs of gratitude and obedience than the bank.

While one might be tempted to exclude organizational situations from
social exchanges, my previous observations suggest such a move would be
disadvantageous. We lose valuable insights into interpersonal relationships
by making an increasingly artificial distinction. Foa and Foa (1974, 1976)
have taken a position that allows examination of economic exchanges as
well as social exchanges, while recognizing the differences between the
two.

These researchers focus their attention on the objects being exchanged and the setting in which the exchange takes place. By doing this, they allow us to study exchanges of money in a family setting and loyalty in a business. Exchanges of various types of resources involve different rules. We will examine the complete list of resources later, but in order to amplify their point, let us examine their analysis of how two extremely different resources are exchanged.

Love and money are typically viewed as two extremely different resources. Our society still enforces sanctions against people who attempt to "buy friends" and formal sanctions against "buying affection" as in the case of prostitution. Exchanges of money for money and love for love involve different rules.

Exchanges involving love and money differ in three ways. First, they create different conditions following the exchange. A person exchanging money has less money after giving it. A person exchanging love may actually have more love to give after the initial exchange. We come to appreciate ourselves more after giving love to another; hence, there is a gain in love after giving love. Giving money generally involves give and take; when one gives money, one generally does not take it as well. However, exchanges of love are ambivalent; one might hate and love at the same time. Money is much easier to barter for in exchange, whereas the need for love is very difficult to express. Indeed, the exchange of money does not even require a face-to-face interaction; by using credit cards, we can exchange money over the phone or through the mails.

In order to exchange affection, it is often necessary to be in the presence of the other party. Many people have encountered the difficulties of maintaining "long distance" love affairs for even short periods of time. Finally, money can be exchanged for a wider variety of resources than love. Money can be used to prompt the exchange of services or goods, whereas love tends to be exchanged for only a few resources. Because of this restriction, love can only be exchanged in a few settings (usually in close interpersonal relationships), whereas money can be exchanged in a greater range of settings.

Second, environmental cues may facilitate or inhibit the exchange of money or love. Generally, considerable time is needed before love is exchanged; because trust is necessary, this resource tends to be given in friendship rather than to strangers. The previous history of interaction as well as the future prospects of exchange become necessary conditions for the exchange of love. Money, on the other hand, requires little time or trust for exchange. Friends as well as strangers can easily make this exchange. Equally relevant for interpersonal communication is the notion that an exchange of love requires more understanding of the other person than the exchange of money. Since love can take many forms, it becomes necessary to understand the form which is most appreciated by the individual recipient. Money takes fewer forms, requires less understanding of the recipient, and may actually be aided by the existence of many people regardless of their relationship to an individual. As such, the exchange of love is more likely to take place with few people, whereas the exchange of money will be facilitated by larger numbers of people.

Third, understanding how a resource is exchanged does not occur all at once, but instead develops gradually. The understanding of how love is negotiated occurs early, whereas the use of money is understood much later. As a result, love and money are best exchanged under conditions similar to those during which the person began to acknowledge the use of the resource. The exchange of love occurs most appropriately under conditions similar to those experienced as a child in a close family. Money is primarily used after a certain point in maturation in which the individual learns to interact with people external to the family. As such, money is most appropriately exchanged with people outside of one's family.

Thus, Foa and Foa recognize that exchange is governed by regularities. The regularities differ according to the resource being exchanged and its relationship to the conditions at the time of its exchange. Instead of excluding certain resources from social exchange, they attempt to recognize their differences and include them in their theory.

At this juncture, we have noted that social exchange involves two people providing each other with objects or activities in a variety of settings. It is important that we note another distinction between types of exchange. Ekeh (1974) extended the work of Levi-Strauss (1969) into a taxonomy of exchange. *Restricted exchange* involves two parties directly benefiting each other but not receiving or giving benefits to any other parties in the situation. Such situations might occur when two people are isolated from others (exclusive restricted exchange) with no potential alternative partners. Some relational partners become so committed to each other that they might not even recognize the existence of other people, let alone think of life without the relational partner. These intense relationships are often called symbiotic relationships (Scheflin, 1972). On the other hand, restricted exchange might involve two people who just happen to be exchanging benefits with each other, but could also exchange with other relational partners (inclusive restricted exchange).

Another form of social exchange described by Ekeh differs from most of the other types of exchange presented by other theorists. *Generalized exchange* involves more than two people; individuals do not receive benefits from the party to whom they have provided benefits. Person A might provide help to person B. Person B provides help to person C, but person B does not reciprocate to person A. This form of generalized exchange is called chain generalized exchange. A different form of generalized exchange occurs when a group of people give to one single individual. At a time of illness, all the members of a family may pull together to provide assistance to the weakened family member. After recovering from the illness, the person may join with other family members to help some other stricken member of the family. This form of generalized exchange is called individual-focused net generalized exchange. Finally, group-focused net generalized exchange might occur. In this case, an individual may reward an entire group of persons. For example, some gourmet clubs operate so that each month one person hosts a dinner for all other members. While the host receives a meal in return, it is as a member of the club, not as a single repayment of the debt.

Restricted and generalized exchange are important distinctions because they operate according to different principles. Restricted exchange is guided by attempts to maintain equality in the exchange. The relational partners avoid debt because of the emotional responses that are created by inequality. We do not like to be obligated to others, nor do we like to have others not .repay their obligations to us. In social systems in which generalized exchange operates, people tend to trust each other. A credit mentality exists in which individuals have faith that they will take care of others and will be taken care of in turn, although not necessarily by the same people. This credit mentality is facilitated by what Ekeh refers to as the Law of Extended Credit. When a person receives aid from one individual, the receiver owes not the specific giver but the overall group of people in the social system. If a person refuses to reciprocate to an individual, everyone in the system suffers. Thus, individuals become less concerned about equality of exchange with a specific other since the entire social system will care for them.

Although not discussed by Ekeh, an interesting conflict emerges when the two types of exchanges collide. For instance, this author has encountered many young marrieds who describe being pressured to have children. Parents and grandparents often drop subtle, and many times blatant, suggestions that the time has come for "new arrivals to the family." This communication is often met with resistance, and consequently both sides of the generation gap feel confused and often angry. It is possible that some understanding of this situation might be gained by applying restricted and generalized exchange. One may view the various generations of a family as being involved in generalized exchange. The older generation sacrificed for their children with little expectation of receiving the same rewards in return. However, the older generation expects their children to sacrifice for future children when the time comes. Depending upon how old the family is, this cycle might have been maintained for many years. The assumption seems to be that sequential sacrifice will lead to betterment of future generations.

For a variety of reasons, married couples are no longer having as many children. Frequently, couples choose not to have children at all, at which point generalized exchange stops. Childless couples may be viewed by older generations as being "selfish" since they are no longer sacrificing for the next generation. The chain of exchange is broken and a host of familial pressures may be brought to bear in order to restore it.

From the view of the newly married, the exchange may not be generalized but purely restricted. The question of having children is not something to be determined by previous generations. Such a decision can only be made within the new family, between husband and wife.

While generalized exchange may certainly impact upon interpersonal communication in an important way, most interpersonal communication situations are restricted and will be treated as such.

The last condition necessary for understanding social exchange is to note that it is generally entered into voluntarily. While persons in a social exchange may believe that they have few alternatives, these restrictions tend to be psychological rather than physical. They occur because the person believes that other alternatives are extremely unlikely to be more rewarding.

In sum, *social exchange is the voluntary transference of some object or activity from one person to another in return for other objects or activities.* Next, we need to determine what activities or objects are exchanged.

What is Exchanged?

The answer to the above question seems quite simple. The definition of social exchange states that objects and activities are exchanged. However, this lacks precision; one is still left wondering exactly what kinds of objects and activities are to be exchanged. This section discusses in more detail these objects and activities.

The first important concept is that exchanges involve *resources*. Foa and Foa (1974) define a resource as any commodity, material or symbolic, which can be transmitted through interpersonal behavior. Of the social exchange theorists, these authors provide the most complete listing and description of these resources. They posit six types: love, status, services, goods, information, and money. Love is the communication of affection, warmth, or comfort. Status is the expression of regard, prestige, or esteem. Services involve activities related to a person's body or belongings. Goods are tangible products, objects, or materials. Information takes the form of advice, opinions, or instructions. Finally, money is defined as coin, currency, or tokens which are endowed with a standard unit of value by the social system.

The types of resources are distinct categories and can be differentiated on two dimensions: particularism and concreteness. Particularism represents the degree of value associated with a resource that stems from the particular person providing it. Love is the most particularistic resource since it gains a great deal of value from the particular person who provides it. Expressions of affection from an attractive partner will be more valued than similar expressions from an unattractive person. Services and status are more particularistic than information, goods, and money, but less so than love. Information and goods are more particularistic than money, but less so than services, status, and love. Money is the least particularistic; its value is unaffected by the giver (assuming it is not counterfeit), and, therefore, it is a universal resource.

Concreteness refers to the specific form the resource takes in exchange. Services and goods are thought to be the most concrete resources since they are easy to observe in the exchange. One performs an activity for another, like fixing a car, or gives some good to another, like delivering a newspaper. Love and money are thought to be moderate in concreteness since they can be exchanged in *both* concrete and symbolic forms. Status and information are least concrete (or most abstract). These resources are transferred most often via communication of symbols. A stated opinion or a compliment can be very valuable to an individual, but the form tends to be restricted to communication rather than transferable as tangible objects or activities.

Emerson (1976: 347) suggests a definition of resource that is complementary to that provided by Foa and Foa. He defines a resource as "an ability, possession, or other attribute of an actor giving him the capacity to reward (or punish) another specified actor." When taken together, the two definitions of resource provide several important insights. First, resources vary in how they are accumulated and stored. Some resources such as money and goods are relatively easy to store and their accumulation can be easily observed. These resources tend to be identified by a person's possessions. If we go to a person's bank or home, we can determine how much money or how many goods are available for exchange.

Other resources such as love, status, services, and information may be defined as abilities rather than possessions, and determining their accumulation is more difficult. Several examples may clarify this distinction. When people receive expressions of affection (love), they may have gained, but what has been received is not as readily apparent to an outside observer as with the accumulation of money. The accumulation of love is more likely to be remembered by the person than recorded in a bank account. Therefore, it is often difficult to determine a person's ability to give this resource in an exchange.

When one compliments another, an exchange of status has taken place, but the accumulation of the resource is probably recorded in memory. Exchanges of this type are based upon ability rather than external possessions. For example, a rather simple but important form of expressing status is to be attentive to what another person is saying. When one is paying close attention to the communication of another, one is admitting that what the person is saying is of some importance. This is true even if we subsequently reject its validity, for we at least admit that the person has a view worth refuting. If we ignore the person we deny the person's existence. Watzlawick, Beavin, and Jackson (1967) have referred to this lack of attention as disconfirmation and hypothesize that it is the ultimate insult. Some parents say to their children in exasperation, "Look at me when I am talking to you!" However, people differ in their ability to be attentive to others. Norton and Pettegrew (1979) suggested that this ability is a part of a person's communicator style. We might hope that students who are communication majors might develop this style. While they may develop the ability, the possession of this resource will not be observable to a potential exchange partner until the beginning of the communication transaction.

The accumulation of services might be equally hidden. Bahr (1976) and Nye and McLaughlin (1976) have demonstrated that perception of a spouse's role competence in providing a variety of services (e.g., child care, emotional support, homemaking) is related to marital satisfaction and power. If this is true, it should be important to an individual to be able to correctly identify a potential spouse's ability in advance of marriage. However, this assessment may be difficult to make. How can we be certain that a person is "good with children" until the person is *with* children?

Finally, the accumulation and storage of information is also relatively unobservable. When people go to a university, they acquire information. The accumulation of information should allow the person to have a great deal of that resource to use in an exchange. However, it is not easy to determine how much information a person has accumulated without relying upon self-report. The person must admit to having a degree in order for us to infer the existence of that resource for exchange.

The second insight from the two definitions stems from whether or not a given resource is rewarding. People desire some resources more than others. These preferred resources might be thought of as rewards. Thibaut and Kelley (1959: 12) define a *reward* as "pleasures, satisfactions, and gratifications the person enjoys." Social exchange theorists assume that rewards serve as positive reinforcements and will increase the probability of behaviors with which they are associated. Of course, not all rewards are valued equally; the more of a resource a person has accumulated, the less valuable that resource becomes to the person.

Blau (1964a) describes six types of social rewards: personal attraction, social acceptance, social approval, instrumental services, respect/prestige, and compliance/power. These are differentiated on the basis of several traits. Rewards such as personal attraction to another, social approval of one's opinions, and respect for one's abilities are typically resources for which there is no bartering. They mean more if they emerge spontaneously. Other rewards such as acceptance into a group, instrumental services, and compliance are subject to negotiation. Giving such resources is often the result of a conscious calculation of a request rather than spontaneous behavior. Rewards might also be distinguished by whether they are intrinsic or external to the association. Rewards such as personal attraction and social approval and instrumental services are conveyed within a relationship but do not exist just because the relationship exists. They are labeled extrinsic rewards. Finally, respect/prestige and compliance/power are characterized as unilateral rewards. When one gives respect, one also bestows superior prestige on the other person. One implicitly tells the other person that his abilities are superior to one's own. A person who complies with another's requests bestows superior power on the other person and sacrifices her own power as a result. Therefore, unilateral rewards entail a direct cost such as loss of prestige or power.

Since some resources are valued by individuals, the loss of these resources should be avoided. A person can lose a valued resource by receiving the obverse of the resource (e.g., hate instead of love, an insult instead of a compliment) or by missing the opportunity for a better exchange. Thus, a *cost* is thought to be the receipt of aversive stimulation *or* rewards one could have gained from another exchange had one entered into it instead of the chosen one. The latter form of cost is referred to as rewards foregone.

Blau (1964a) divides costs into three types. *Investment costs* represent the time and effort a person commits toward acquiring the skills to provide resources to another. A person may invest a significant amount of time and money in obtaining a college degree to obtain resources such as information. *Direct costs* represent the resources one gives to another in an exchange. When a person gives money to another, the direct cost is the amount given. As noted by Foa and Foa earlier, some resources may not involve as much direct cost as others (e.g., love given often increases gains in love through self-appreciation). *Opportunity costs* represent the rewards foregone from other possible exchanges one missed by engaging in the chosen one.

Thus, social exchange involves the transference of resources. Some resources are valued and are considered rewards. The loss or denial of these rewards is considered a cost. Now, the next important question concerns why exchange takes place.

Why Do We Engage In Social Exchange?

While stated somewhat differently in each of the Social Exchange Theories, the guiding force of social exchange is self-interest. For Homans (1961), social exchange is guided by the pursuit of profit or rewards minus costs. Thibaut and Kelley (1959) argue that people are seeking "goodness of outcomes" or a situation involving high rewards and low costs. Walster, Berscheid, and Walster (1976: 2) bluntly state this assumption: "Equity theory, too, assumes that man is selfish." People engaged in social exchange transfer resources in a manner consistent with their self-interest. *Self-interest is defined as the tendency to seek preferred resources from others.*

Four points are critical to this notion of self-interest. First, this conception assumes that self-interest can be malevolent or benevolent. Certainly, some individuals do seek profitable exchange in which they are only concerned with maximizing rewards and minimizing costs, regardless of the profits of others. Rubin and Brown (1975) suggest that such bargainers have individualistic motives; the profit or loss of others is irrelevant to them. Only their own outcomes matter.

Other individuals seek a fair exchange when they become concerned not just with their own rewards and costs but also the rewards and costs of others. Rubin and Brown describe bargainers who have cooperative motives in which they seek to maximize *joint profits* rather than just their own profit. However, a dark side of a fair exchange might be represented by what Rubin and Brown call the competitive motive, where persons seek to maximize their own rewards and at the same time do better than others. We might expect, though, that most exchanges are guided by a cooperative motive and the establishment of equity (Adams, 1965) rather than a competitive or individualistic motive and the resultant one-sided outcomes. This author once confronted a student who said that she willingly accepted rewards from others with no commitment to establishing an equitable exchange with them. After conversing with her, I found that she had a large quantity of resources but an even longer list of *former* friends! People will, if given a choice, leave inequitable relationships.

Second, this conception assumes that people may or may not be aware of the best way to fulfill their self-interest. As noted by Heath (1976), people often make decisions in exchange situations based on inaccurate or incomplete information. Therefore, to outside observers, the course of action chosen may not seem to be maximally in their self-interest. However, the individual may think it is.

Third, this conception assumes that people vary in their premeditated behavior. Argyle's (1975) Social Skills Model assumes that planning only takes place at higher levels of behavior in which time is available for forecasting outcomes. A person may preplan a date if given sufficient time. However, ongoing interaction may occur spontaneously with little time for forethought. In such cases, the person's reactions may be so instantaneous as to preclude recall of the reasons for the choice to engage in a given behavior.

Fourth, this notion assumes that self-interest may change. As people change their attitudes or environments, their self-interest may also change. Recently, this author heard a group of women describe why their marriages failed. In each case, the women said their spouses did not meet their needs. Interestingly, the women admitted after questioning that, *at the time* of their marriage, they thought the men would meet their needs. As our desires change, so might our relational partners.

Thus, social exchange involves the voluntary transference of resources by one person to another in order to receive a resource. This exchange is guided by self-interest, which is the tendency to seek rewards from others. It may result in a desire to maximize one's own rewards minus costs or a consideration of one's rewards and costs in relation to the other's rewards and costs. Next, we examine some theories of interpersonal communication.

INTERPERSONAL COMMUNICATION

To some, defining interpersonal communication may seem like a worthless task. "After all, everyone does it so we must know what it is." This author had a student complain about an interpersonal communication class because it was all "common sense." After failing the midterm, she humbly admitted that she saw no need to study something she already "knew." As a result of this new and painful experience, she came to understand that "common sense" is not always an accurate measure of reality, and that we often engage in interpersonal communication processes of which we have little self-awareness. Therefore, it *is* necessary to examine the concept. To explore interpersonal communication, we will examine four statements which characterize it.

First, interpersonal communication occurs in a relational context. In fact, the concepts relationship and interpersonal communication have been typically defined in such a way so as to make them conceptually the same. McCall (1970) has defined a relationship as the substantial probability of interaction between two people. A social relationship exists when two people interact because they view themselves as being the sole members of a common collectivity which causes them to interact in a specific manner. We know that a person has a relationship with another person because they are very likely to communicate with one another. The way they communicate is determined by relational constraints.

The relational constraints stem from at least two sources. The two people view themselves as being the sole members of the relationship. As such, they establish boundary rules to filter out certain other inputs into the relationship (e.g., other people) as well as outputs from the relationship (e.g., the willingness to discuss the relational concerns with others). While a relationship is generally viewed as being somewhat exclusive, some are less so than others. Some merchant-customer relationships may not be as exclusive as others, since many competing relational partners are available.

Now, in addition to exclusivity restraints, relationships may also be constrained by how the people know each other. Some relationships are thought to be role-oriented. The relational partners behave toward each other based upon the roles the other person plays as well as the role the individual has adopted. McCall (1970) has referred to these as formal relationships. McCall and Simmons (1978) have described another form of relationship in which the individuals know each other as distinctive individuals in addition to roles. Such relationships are referred to as interpersonal relationships. Both relationships provide constraints as to the form of communication involved. In a formal relationship, the constraints arise from the specific obligations of the relational roles. In an interpersonal relationship, the constraints stem from our understanding of the other person's specific, individual traits.

The second characteristic of interpersonal communication is that it is guided by knowledge of one's relational partner. Miller and Steinberg (1975) base their conceptualization of interpersonal communication on the types of information relational partners use to make communication predictions about one another. They argue that communication predictions may be based upon cultural, sociological, and psychological information. Cultural information is garnered from the culture to which a person belongs. Sociological information stems from one's group memberships. These first two types of information are very generalized and seem akin to the role-related constraints discussed by McCall. When two people base their communication predictions about each other on cultural or sociological information, their communication is thought to be noninterpersonal. Psychological information comes from understanding the uniqueness of the individual rather than from the person's role. One might infer that information about an individual's personality gives us more accurate assessments about the person than her role. Communication based primarily on psychological information is defined as interpersonal.

One might guess that the predominant type of communication in a relationship may determine the nature of the relationship. People who share cultural and sociological information are limited to engaging in noninterpersonal communication, and, therefore their relationship may be formalized or role-based. People who share psychological as well as cultural and sociological information communicate primarily on an interpersonal level and their relationship may also be described as interpersonal.

The third statement characterizing interpersonal communication is that interpersonal communication involves the transmission of various types of symbols. Given that communication is based upon different types of information, we should find it reflected in the symbolic codes used by relational partners. While not often noted as an interpersonal communication scholar, Basil Bernstein (1975) has developed a taxonomy of language codes that are used.

One type of code is called a lexical restricted code. This type of code is typically ritualistic and highly predictable from person to person. An example might be the kind of "cocktail chatter" one often observes at parties. Some people avoid cocktail parties because the conversation is rather predictable and boring. People tend to discuss the same things: the weather, children, and work. If the people are new acquaintances, the conversation is even more superficial. One might expect that such codes are typically associated with formal, role relationships.

Another code is called an elaborated code, which involves the expression of intent and the disclosure of individual characteristics of the source. We might expect that these codes are used when two people are seeking to better understand each other. The range of topics may increase and the type of information exchanged is more intimate.

The remaining code is called restricted syntactical. Whereas a lexical restricted code is highly ritualized across relationships, a restricted syntactical code is ritualized only within a relationship. In both restricted codes, there is a low likelihood of expressing intent or individual characteristics, but for different reasons. In the case of a lexical restricted code, the people of the culture have no desire to communicate intent and are simply following a cultural ritual. People using a restricted syntactical code understand each other very well because of their relationship. There is no need for communication of intent because it is understood. People who are not part of the relationship may not be able to understand the restricted syntactical code unless they spend a great deal of time observing the relational partners. Therefore, we might find that close interpersonal relationships only use the restricted syntactical code.

The fourth characteristic of interpersonal communication is that it is functional; it serves some purpose. Some have argued that the purpose of interpersonal communication is to help people control their environment (Miller and Steinberg, 1975), and others have argued that it validates our self-concept (Cushman and Craig, 1976). Still others have pointed to how interpersonal communication helps us to meet our needs (Scott and Powers, 1978).

Despite differences in terminology, these scholars are suggesting that people design their interpersonal communication to attain some goal. However, it should be noted that not every interpersonal communication sequence is preplanned (see Berger and Roloff, 1980). Much communication is spontaneous. Despite this caveat, we should find that when interpersonal communication is preplanned, it is designed to serve some purpose. At this juncture we have explored social exchange and interpersonal communication separately from each other. Now it is important to relate them.

INTERPERSONAL COMMUNICATION AS SOCIAL EXCHANGE

Having reviewed the basic concepts, we suggest the following: *Interpersonal communication is a symbolic process by which two people, bound together in a relationship, provide each other with resources or negotiate the exchange of resources.*

Such a statement requires a slightly different definition of the term relationship. Elsewhere, I have defined a relationship as a "mutual agreement, implicit or explicit, between people to interact in order to maximize rewards" (Roloff, 1976: 182). In other words, the focus of a relationship is the attainment of positively valued resources, and communication becomes related to that goal.

Communication is related to the attainment of rewards in two ways. First, communication may be a resource to be exchanged for other goods. Foa and Foa (1974) noted that a variety of resources are provided through communication (e.g., love, status, information). Brock (1968) suggested that information might be thought of as a commodity to be exchanged for compliance. In general, people are more likely to believe, and therefore comply with, information that they believe is unavailable to others. Thus, a communicator might be advised to do the following: (1) create the impression that very few people know about the information being sent to a receiver; (2) increase the effort of the receiver to obtain the information from the source or to understand the message; (3) put restrictions on the further transmission of the information to others; and (4) appear to be reluctant to send the message to the receiver. In all these cases, the information should be perceived by the receiver as scarce, and actual receipt of the information may prompt greater compliance.

A second way in which communication is related to gaining relational rewards is that it can be used to negotiate the condition of future exchanges or to seek redress for previous inequitable exchanges. Rather than being an end in and of itself, communication might also be a means to an end. Recently, Tedeschi and Rosenfeld (1980) pointed out the importance of communication in bargaining and negotiation. Communication allows determination of another's bargaining aspirations, alteration of those aspirations, and provision to the other person of information about our own bargaining goals. While bargaining is not always associated with interpersonal communication, some social exchange theorists have noted its importance to the conduct of interpersonal relationships (Scanzoni, 1972).

In summary, we have explored three areas in this chapter. First, social exchange was defined as the voluntary transference of some objects or activities (resources) from one person to another in return for other objects or activities (resources). Some resources provide pleasures, satisfaction, and gratifications and are referred to as rewards. When one has lost or been denied a reward, that person has experienced a cost. People engage in social exchange to gain rewards from others or, in other words, it is in their own self-interest to exchange with others.

Second, interpersonal communication is the transmission of symbols between relational partners. These symbols are chosen based upon our understanding of our relational partners and because they are anticipated to be functional.

Third, interpersonal communication is a symbolic process by which two people bound together in a relationship provide each other with resources or negotiate the exchange of resources.

2

FIVE APPROACHES
Social Exchange Theory

While the term "Social Exchange Theory" implies the existence of a single theory of exchange, there are actually five
social exchange perspectives: Homans' Operant Psychology
Approach; Blau's Economic Approach; Thibaut and Kelley's
Theory of Interdependence; Foa and Foa's Resource Theory,
and Walster, Berscheid, and Walster's Equity Theory. This
chapter will examine the underlying assumptions of each of
the theories and describe how they view decision-making and
exchange patterns.

There is nothing so practical as a good theory.

Kurt Lewin

Most social scientists heartily agree with Lewin's statement. Theories allow
us to explain previous events and predict their future occurrence. In
addition, they allow people to control environmental forces and, it is
hoped, to improve their lot in life. However, less consensus is found as to
what constitutes a theory. Some scholars use the term to describe untested
hypotheses, vague conceptualizations, or prescriptions. Others insist that a
theory refers to a set of propositions relating concepts to each other from
which hypotheses can be logically deduced and empirically tested.

Because the academic community differs in definition, not all Social
Exchange Theories meet the requirements for theory. For example,
Homans (1961, 1974) presents a formalized theory which attempts to
meet the requirements of deduction, but Blau (1964a) does not attempt to
develop propositions that constitute his theory. Indeed, the term theory

must be defined broadly so as to incorporate all perspectives. In this book, a theory is defined as a set of statements characterizing some phenomena from which hypotheses might be generated.

While the approaches described in this chapter differ in form, they do provide information about three things. First, they all describe their underlying assumptions or starting points. Some base their theoretical framework on psychological theories (e.g., Homans, 1961, 1974; Thibaut and Kelley, 1959; and Foa and Foa, 1974), while others find their origins primarily in economics (Blau, 1964a) or other social exchange perspectives (Walster, Berscheid, and Walster, 1976). Second, the Social Exchange Theories describe the influences on human behavior. Roughly speaking, each describes the decision-making processes that lead to behavior. Third, they provide explanations of exchange patterns found in interpersonal relationships. These patterns represent the accommodation of self-interest by the two parties involved in the relationship.

Therefore, the description of each theory is subdivided into three sections: underlying theoretical base, decision-making, and exchange patterns.

HOMANS' OPERANT PSYCHOLOGY APPROACH

Homans' theory is probably the most well known of the five approaches. His initial journal article (Homans, 1958) and the two editions of his book, *Social Behavior: Its Elementary Forms* (Homans, 1961, 1974) are primary sources. While Homans' theory is the most familiar, it is also the most controversial of the five theories. Many authors have critically evaluated the applicability of his theory to sociological phenomena.[1] Emerson (1969, 1972a, b) has attempted to formalize and extend Homans' analysis using the rules of formal logic.

Underlying Theoretical Base

As noted earlier, Homans' perspective has generated a great deal of debate in sociology. Most of this controversy stems from his underlying theoretical base. While Homans is a sociologist, he primarily relies upon behaviorist psychology to build his exchange theory.[2] Specifically, the work of B. F. Skinner provides the stimulus for much of Homans' thinking.

A brief explanation of Skinner's position will provide insight into the critical reactions to Homans. Skinner (1974) suggests four assumptions regarding human behavior. First, a person is an organism which inhabits the earth with other organisms. Human beings possess unique anatomical and physiological characteristics that have evolved as their ancestors adapted to their environments. Those which aided survival have passed onward while those which inhibited survival have not. These characteristics make up our genetic endowment. Second, a newborn human being becomes a "person" when learning to behave in a fashion that has been reinforced by other people. Third, human behavior is under the control of cues in the setting in which the behavior takes place. Finally, the ability of human beings to learn to engage in behaviors is part of the genetic endowment.

Because Skinner asserts that environmental stimuli cause human behavior, one might assume that cognitive processes (e.g., thought, attitudes) play no role in his approach. A person might be conceptualized as a relatively passive, mindless entity buffeted about by the environment. While some forms of behaviorism do downplay the importance of cognitive processes (see Day, 1975), Skinner acknowledges their existence and describes their relationship to behavior.

To Skinner, thinking is covert behavior. When a person is thinking, this process might also include monitoring feelings and future actions. For example, before a date, a person might preplan conversations, places to go, and things to do. In such cases, Skinner argues that thinking is simply part of the larger behavioral sequence of going out on a date; the anticipation of behavioral outcomes. During the date, the person may ponder: "Am I having a good time? What should I say next?" Whether before or during the date, thinking was caused by environmental cues. Before the date, the person was reacting to the arrangement made with the other person. The other person caused the thought process to orient toward future interaction. During the date, the person was reacting to internal feelings caused by the other person or setting. In any case, thought occurred as an effect of external cues and while it helped control behavior, it did not *cause* behavior. Thought was a covert behavioral reaction to an external stimuli just as the overt behaviors (e.g., talking, dancing) were outward reactions to the same stimuli.

Skinner does not ignore cognitive processes, he just does not assume that they cause behavior. They are simply another form of behavioral response to external stimuli. However, when one considers that cognitive processes play a central role in most of our theorizing (see Langer, 1978), even a reduced role becomes controversial and leads to an overexaggerated feeling that Skinner is describing a robot rather than oneself.

Another criticism emanates not from Skinner's theory but from methods associated with it. People associate behaviorism with the "Skinner Box" and white rats. Understandably, most people do not want to admit they have anything in common with rodents, including behavioral regularities. In his own defense, Skinner (1974: 226) writes, "The reign of the white rat in the psychological laboratory ended at least a quarter of a century ago." However, critics of his approach are still likely to assert that the findings are not applicable beyond laboratory animals.

While a variety of other indictments of Skinner's approach have been made (see, Mischel, 1975), the few described here suggest a problem for Homans. While he may feel secure using behaviorist psychology as a base upon which to build his theory, critics may view it as a base of quicksand rather than concrete.

Decision-Making

Homans' analysis of human behavior is based on principles of operant conditioning: people repeat behavior that is rewarded and do not repeat behaviors that are punished. To elaborate, Homans (1974) describes five propositions.

The first proposition is called the success proposition and states, "For all actions taken by persons, the more often a particular action of a person is rewarded, the more likely the person is to perform that action" (Homans, 1974: 16). This proposition simply suggests that people will tend to repeat actions that result in reward attainment. Homans does note limits to this proposition. Research suggests that organisms (human or otherwise) tend to repeat a behavior more frequently when it is rewarded irregularly (variable-ratio schedules of reinforcement) than when the behavior is rewarded regularly (fixed-ratio schedules of reinforcement). However, Homans asserts that the proposition is generally true.

The second proposition is the stimulus proposition and states, "If in the past the occurrence of a particular stimulus, or set of stimuli, has been the occasion on which a person's action has been rewarded, then the more similar the present stimuli are to the past ones, the more likely the person is to perform the action, or some similar action, now" (Homans, 1974: 22-23). This proposition describes stimulus generalization. In a marriage, a spouse may choose to employ a persuasive strategy found successful in similar circumstances in the past. The similar circumstance could be defined by the topic, the spouse, time, or any environmental cue salient in *both* situations.

The third proposition is the value proposition and states, "The more valuable to a person is the result of his action, the more likely he is to perform the action" (Homans, 1974: 25). Value refers to how rewarding a resource is. Homans assumes that resources take on varying degrees of value, just as the denial of a resource can vary in degree of punishment. While he is not precise as to the value attached to various resources, he does suggest that value may come from two sources. Some resources are innately valued; we are born needing them. We value food and shelter because of their absolute importance to survival. Other resources acquire value through their association with the attainment of other rewards. Money is valued because of its ability to be exchanged for innately valued resources such as food or shelter. Indeed, Homans has suggested that some resources such as money and social approval are so necessary for attaining our needs that their value is generalized across people in the society.

The fourth proposition is the deprivation-satiation proposition and states, "The more often in the recent past a person has received a particular reward, the less valuable any further unit of that reward becomes for him" (Homans, 1974: 29). This proposition sets a limit on the success proposition. There is a point at which a person no longer needs any more of a given resource. At that point, any further unit of that resource will not have as great an effect on the repetition of a behavior.

The fifth proposition is the aggression/approval proposition and has two parts: "(1) When a person's action does not receive the reward he expected, or receives punishment he did not expect, he will be angry; he becomes more likely to perform aggressive behavior, and the results of such behavior become more valuable to him" (Homans, 1974: 37). (2) "When a person's action receives rewards he expected, especially a greater reward than he expected, or does not receive punishment he expected, he will be pleased; he becomes more likely to perform approving behavior, and the results of such behavior become more valuable to him" (Homans, 1974: 39). Homans is suggesting that after a period of time an individual can anticipate that certain rewards or punishments will follow particular behaviors. A person who does not receive the anticipated reward becomes frustrated, and the frustration automatically elicits aggression which, if successful in attaining rewards, becomes more probable in similar situations in the future. A child who receives a candy sucker during each visit to the grocery store will come to associate shopping with reward attainment. Should the mother or father forget to buy the candy, the child may become frustrated and a "temper tantrum" will result. To the extent that the tantrum results in the child receiving candy, the aggressive behavior has been reinforced and should be repeated in similar circumstances in the future.

On the other hand, Homans suggests that if we are consistently punished or not rewarded in a situation, we will also anticipate those outcomes in similar settings. Rather than aggression, the violation of these anticipations results in relief or satisfaction. The child who unexpectedly receives ice cream instead of candy while shopping with mother should become (at least while eating the ice cream) more obedient and happy. The child should also come to expect ice cream on future shopping trips.

These five propositions form the base of Homans' theory. They appear in both editions of *Social Behavior*, although in slightly altered forms. The central idea is that a person's behavior can be predicted from knowledge of the outcomes produced by a behavior in previous settings. The person is somewhat trapped by reinforcements received in the past. Previous history of reinforcement in similar situations should be a major determinant of current behavior. If the person recognizes cues in the current setting which are similar to those in previous situations, then previously reinforced behavior should automatically follow.

In the second edition of *Social Behavior*, Homans added a sixth proposition which summarizes propositions 1, 2, and 3. This proposition is entitled the rationality proposition and states, "In choosing between alternative actions, a person will choose that one for which, as perceived by him at the time, the value, V, of the result, multiplied by the probability, p, of getting the result, is the greater" (Homans, 1974: 43). A human being choosing between alternative behaviors is most likely to engage in the behavior which has consistently resulted in resources of greatest value in similar situations. While this proposition seems to imply that choices are determined by some mentalistic process, Homans does not mean this. The choice of an alternative is not determined by the individual, but by previous reinforcement schedules. In fact, if we had complete information about a person's history of reinforcements in similar situations, we should be able to predict current behavior as well as the person can. Since behaviorism does not assume that a person is always consciously calculating rewards and costs of a behavior, an outside observer with perfect information about a person's previous history should be better able to predict a person's behavior than the person can.

Homans presents a set of interrelated propositions arising from behavioristic psychology. Homans is a reductionist. He believes that all forms of behavior, regardless of complexity, may be reduced to these propositions, and that these six propositions can explain interpersonal behavior.

Exchange Patterns

Homans has described a person who is seeking positive stimulation from the current setting: a person who does whatever has "worked in the past," a profit-seeker. When dealing with inanimate objects, profit seeking involves giving up something in the pursuit of some positive valued resource. A person cooking supper might decide whether the time, effort, and money expended on preparing the food is worth the satisfaction received from eating it. In one sense, such an exchange is somewhat easy, since the cook is active and the food is relatively passive. Once cooking skill is perfected and assuming relatively good cooking instruments and ingredients, the outcomes of supper should be relatively stable and satisfying.

However, when two people are in an exchange relationship, complexity emerges. The other environmental cue is active and makes choices based on previous histories of reinforcements. Since these schedules are not obvious, the exchange becomes problematic. The person may not respond as we wish unless provided with sufficient rewards, and we do not always know what those rewards ought to be.

Homans (1961: 62) recognizes the importance of the other person in the exchange relationship when he writes: "The open secret of human exchange is to give the other man behavior that is more valuable to him than it is costly to you and to get from him behavior that is more valuable to you than it is costly to him." Thus, a person gives something worthwhile to another in order to get something worthwhile in return. However, how does one determine the fairness of such an exchange?

Based on the works of Aristotle, Homans (1961: 75) argues that fairness is determined by the rule of distributive justice. The rule states: "A man in an exchange relation with another will expect that the rewards of each man be proportional to his costs—the greater the rewards the greater the costs—and that the net rewards, or profits, of each man be proportional to his investments—the greater the investments the greater the profits." The term investment refers to the time and effort put into an activity or job. Thus, a married couple of equal investment (age, number of years married) should expect to receive from each other resources of equal value resulting in equal profit.

Should an unfair exchange occur, Homans predicts the parties will feel distressed. He (1961: 75) states: "The more to a man's disadvantage the rule of distributive justice fails of realization, the more likely he is to display the emotional behavior we call anger." However, when a person gains from the violation of the rule (gets proportionately more rewards than someone with equal investment), Homans predicts the person might feel guilty. While his prediction is quite noble, he does suggest that people might just as easily rationalize away the guilt.

The propositions describing decision-making are still applicable to the exchange of resources between two people. A different interpretation is necessary for the individuals in the exchange. They may respond to reinforcement automatically based upon their prior histories, but they must respond with a resource that fits into another's reinforcement history as well. These people are bound together based upon their history of exchanging resources with each other that conform to their mutual self-interests.

BLAU'S ECONOMIC APPROACH

Blau generated an exchange perspective that extends the analysis by Homans. *Exchange and Power in Everyday Life* (Blau, 1964a) and two of his articles (Blau, 1964b, 1968) are primary sources for his approach. While Blau has not created as much controversy as Homans, a number of scholars have critically evaluated his approach to sociological phenomena (e.g., Bierstedt, 1965; MacIntyre, 1967; Heath, 1968a, b; Mulkay, 1971; Ekeh, 1974; Turner, 1974; Chadwick-Jones, 1976; Heath, 1976; Mitchell, 1978).

Underlying Theoretical Base

Generally, scholars have been less critical of Blau than of Homans. Part of this acceptance is due to Blau's recognition of emergent properties as controllers of social exchange, and his reliance upon economic principles rather than operant psychology as a theoretical base.

As noted in the previous section, Homans is a reductionist. He believes that all complex behaviors can be reduced to the propositions of his theory. This position has not met with universal acclamation and heated debate on this point has ensued (see Homans, 1967; Blain, 1971a, b; Homans, 1971b, c; Chadwick-Jones, 1973; Ekeh, 1974 for examples of this debate).

Blau has avoided controversy by recognizing that properties emerge that cannot be explained by the individual reinforcement histories of the participants. He does not reject the validity of operant psychology but states that it cannot account for all the phenomena involved in an interpersonal exchange, i.e., emergent properties.

According to Blau (1964a: 3), emergent properties "are essentially relationships between elements in a structure. The relationships are not contained in the elements, though they could not exist without them, and they define the structure." For example, the emergent property in an interpersonal social exchange is the relationship between the two partners. The nature of the agreement may not be apparent from the exact reinforcement histories of the two relational partners. Two people may engage in certain interpersonal behaviors with each other because they have been rewarded for doing so in the past. Unless they each find the other's response rewarding, they may not be able to continue with their desired behavior. A person may have found housework to be associated with punishments. Therefore, we would expect the reinforcement history to cause active avoidance of such behaviors. However, in order to maintain a certain relationship with another, it may be required that chores be shared. People may develop agreements for reward distribution that are not obvious from their reinforcement histories. The agreements may even be based on anticipated rewards rather than previously received ones. The person trusts the other to provide promised rewards because of previous history of exchanges.

Blau's approach uses economics as a primary underlying theoretical base. While Homans discusses economics, he primarily operates from the perspective of operant psychology; on the other hand, Blau recognizes the importance of operant psychology but prefers to build primarily upon economics.

As noted in Chapter 1 of this book, Blau sees several important differences between social and economic exchange. These differences stem primarily from the informal and unspecified nature of social exchange. Despite these differences, Blau believes that methods used to describe economic principles (e.g., indifference curves, supply and demand curves) can be used to derive testable hypotheses about social exchange. He uses these methods to predict how advice might be exchanged for compliance in work groups. Nord (1969) has constructed a similar analysis of the exchange of social approval and conformity in a group.

While most critics applaud Blau's use of economic methods, problems have not gone unnoticed. Heath (1968a, 1976) has described some minor errors in Blau's descriptions of the various curves, and, more importantly, has questioned whether we can meet the mathematical assumptions of the economic models when we examine social exchanges. Our measurement of social rewards may be at odds with the requirements of the economic models, and the nature of some social rewards may simply be different than those of economic commodities. Therefore, Blau's use of economic methods may provide a useful analogy but may not be able to provide the exact predictions we find in economics.

Decision-Making

Blau's analysis of how people decide upon a behavior is based upon a person's expectations. He writes (1964a: 18), "The only assumption made is that human beings choose between alternative potential associates or courses of action by evaluating the experiences or expected experiences with each in terms of a preference ranking and then selecting the best alternative." A person estimates the potential for gain from an activity or person, compares it with other alternatives, and chooses the alternative which is expected to provide the greatest profit.

Blau has also described three types of expectations that will influence a person's decisions: general, particular, and comparative. General expectations are those rewards a person thinks are available in various aspects of life: income and fringe benefits associated with one's occupation, or emotional support and affection from one's friends. Blau suggests that these general expectations range from some minimum level below which dissatisfaction is felt to some maximum level representing an ideal amount. General expectations are thought to be formed by social norms of what a person ought to receive and the previous level of reward attained by that individual.

Particular expectations are rewards received from another person. These include the anticipation that another's behavior will conform to social standards of conduct and will provide more or less rewards compared with associating with other people.

Comparative expectations include an analysis of rewards received from a relationship minus costs of maintaining the relationship. This difference defines the person's profit, and Blau assumes that the more profitable a relationship, the more committed the person is to it.

These expectations influence the person's desire for social rewards. Blau assumes that as a person gains a certain level of reward, the individual needs at least that level to remain satisfied. In other words, minimum satisfactory level of reward is defined by current level of rewards. In addition, Blau argues that the attainment of a level of reward that meets a person's expectation is more satisfying than levels that go beyond the expectation. In economics, this notion is referred to as diminishing marginal utility. Homans described this concept in his deprivation-satiation proposition. The more a person has received a resource in the recent past, the less of that resource is needed now. Finally, Blau suggests the more costly or scarce a resource, the more a person will value that resource.

In one respect, Blau's analysis is similar to Homans'. A person considers the possible outcomes of the alternatives and chooses the one which is most likely to be profitable. However, an important difference should be noted. Homans assumes that people can only choose alternatives which have been rewarded in similar situations in the past. The current situation provides cues causing the person to engage in rewarded behavior. While Blau assumes that previous reinforcement histories are important, he concedes that they are not totally constraining. Expectations arising from the relationship with the other or from social norms may influence the choice as much or more than previous reinforcement. Indeed, a person may choose to suffer current costs in the anticipation of future gains. This delayed gratification is not something we would expect from Homans' approach.

Exchange Patterns

Blau recognizes the importance of emergent properties to social exchange. In this section, we see how these emergent properties are reflected in exchange patterns, and focus on two general positions taken by Blau with regard to exchange patterns.

First, Blau argues that social exchange is influenced by the nature of the relationship between two individuals, and that relationships develop along with social exchange. When a person offers a reward to another for the first time, the relationship begins. If this reward is accepted, the receiver is obligated to the giver. The giver, in turn, has taken a risk. The receiver may choose not to repay the obligation to the loss of the giver. However, the receiver may wish to continue the relationship and will in some way repay the debt. As the debt is repaid, the original giver may be prompted to provide more of the reward, and the relationship grows. Thus, as obligations are incurred and repaid, partners come to trust one another, which facilitates further exchange. If an obligation is not repaid or if a reward is not accepted, we might expect that the relationship will be one of distrust and further exchanges avoided.

Second, social context influences the exchange. For example, the roles that a person plays will affect opportunities for exchange with others and costs. Scanzoni (1972) argues that traditional marital roles provide men with greater opportunities for rewards than women. In particular, husbands who work outside the home have greater access to income and relationships than wives who do not work outside the home. Therefore, a housewife may come to view her relationship with her husband as being very costly. Her acquaintance with other people as well as her income may be limited by staying at home, causing her opportunity costs to increase.

Thus, roles and their resultant opportunity costs influence our potential for profit in an exchange.

Social context also includes norms that guide exchange. Groups typically create norms which suggest how exchanges should be conducted. Two concepts are important to this analysis. First, Blau argues that the supply and demand for resources can be thought to affect the "going rate of exchange" between two resources. If someone has a high need for affection and friendship but has limited numbers of contacts, then that person may be very willing to exchange valued resources with the available partners in order to meet these needs. Thus, the going rate gives us some notion of the relative value of two resources. The going rate is not reflective of any moral judgment of how the resources *should* be related to each other. Second, social groups also develop norms that indicate what should be a "fair rate of exchange." These notions of fair exchange are generally related to the investments a person has made to supply rewarding services to the community. Assuming that families are valued by our society, a person who has invested a great deal of time raising a family ought to receive greater resources than a person with no family. However, Blau noted that the going rate and the fair rate may not be consistent. Our society may have a long-term commitment to families, but as the supply of families depletes the available demand, a person with long-term commitments to the family may find fewer rewards than a person with fewer family commitments.

Blau also suggests that norms of fair exchange are often enforced by informal sanctions against violators. A person who grossly violates the fair exchange may expect some social disapproval, even though the going rate has not been valued.

Power differences are also part of the social context which influences exchange. A person who monopolizes a large number of valued resources may be able to violate the fair rate of exchange with some impudence. Unless people are able to engage in reciprocal exchange, obtain resources from a variety of sources, take resources by force, or do without them, then they may be compelled to exchange at levels that are lower than those specified by the fair exchange.

A final influence of the social context stems from interrelated exchange relationships. Some exchanges can only be understood by looking at their impact on other relationships. When two people marry, they may find that they not only have solidified their relationship but also have solidified a number of other relationships: e.g., in-law relationships. A newlywed may appear to be very understanding in the face of indifference or abuse from in-laws. The person seems to be uninterested in profit while providing rewards in the face of rising costs. However, this exchange may be profitable if the behavior can be explained by the desire not to alienate one's spouse. Indeed, fighting with in-laws may be an excellent way to disrupt the marital exchange relationship.

Blau moves beyond the principles of operant psychology to embrace concepts in economics. His perspective still argues that people base their behavior on the anticipation of profit, but recognizes that emergent properties defined by their relationship and the surrounding social structure influence the exchange as well.

THIBAUT AND KELLEY'S THEORY OF INTERDEPENDENCE[3]

While Homans and Blau are sociologists, Thibaut and Kelley find their academic home in social psychology. Their theory has been updated and extended beyond its original scope (Thibaut and Kelley's *The Social Psychology of Groups*, 1959; Kelley and Thibaut's *Interpersonal Relations*, 1978; and Kelley's *Personal Relationships*, 1979). Extensions and critiques of their work are available (Deutsch and Krauss, 1965; Jones and Gerard, 1967; Gergen, 1969; Simpson, 1972; Swensen, 1973; Secord and Backman, 1974; Heath, 1976; Chadwick-Jones, 1976).

Underlying Theoretical Base

Thibaut and Kelley base their theory on two conceptualizations: drive reduction and gaming principles. Like Homans and Blau, Thibaut and Kelley argue that people seek reinforcements. In fact, they state this principle (1959: 5) as a primary assumption of the theory. "We accept as a basic premise that most socially significant behavior will not be repeated unless it is reinforced, rewarded in some way." To be rewarded means that a person has undergone drive reduction or need fulfillment. This is consistent with a set of theories called Activation Theory (see Berkowitz, 1969). Quite simply, this approach assumes that some internal drive mechanism prompts behavior. The reduction of this drive is pleasurable, and stimuli associated with drive reduction become capable of evoking pleasure and therefore become rewarding in and of themselves. Thus, social exchange involves processes by which two people provide mutual resources that reduce drives or fulfill each other's needs.

Because the principles of drive reduction tend to be descriptive of a single individual, Thibaut and Kelley developed a second set of principles to describe social exchange between two people, i.e., gaming principles.

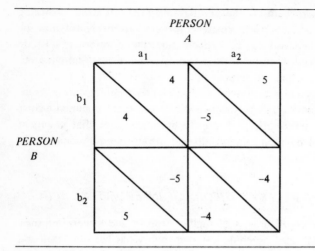

FIGURE 1   A Two-Person Mixed-Motive Game Matrix

Game Theory specifies the ideal way two people might go about resolving a conflict given certain antecedent conditions. These conditions include the following: (1) each partner in a conflict attempts to maximize personal gains and minimize personal losses; (2) each partner knows what the other person's outcomes are as well as his own; (3) no communication occurs between partners so that each person is uncertain as to what the other person will do; (4) each person's outcomes are dependent upon the behavior of the other person as well as her own choice; and (5) the outcomes of a conflict are easily measured and their values fixed.

The means of specifying the ideal moves of the opponents involves studying choices in games. A variety of games exists which might be applied to interpersonal relationships (see Swensen, 1973; Tedeschi, Schlenker, and Bonoma, 1973; and Steinfatt and Miller, 1974). The most popular is called a two-person mixed-motive game. Figure 1 includes the outcomes of the game in a matrix form. Two people, arbitrarily labeled A and B, are involved in an exchange in which each has two alternative behaviors from which to choose. The numbers in the cells represent the magnitude of reward that each will receive if both choose that cell. The values on the lower left accrue to B and those on the upper right to A. For example, if A chooses to engage in a_1 and B chooses to engage in b_1 then both players receive rewards totaling 4. If, however, A chooses a_2 and B chooses b_1 then A receives rewards totaling 5 and B receives rewards totaling -5. In other words, A gains and B loses in this cell.

While Thibaut and Kelley find the use of game matrices useful for studying interpersonal exchanges, they do not find all of the assumptions of Game Theory to be relevant. Indeed, they argue that actual social exchanges typically involve uncertainty as to another's and one's own outcomes from an exchange, communication between partners about what each will do, and rewards that vary in value as the person receives more or less of them (diminishing marginal utility). Therefore, Thibaut and Kelley use gaming principles as an analogy for analyzing social exchange rather than as a model capable of predicting exact behaviors and outcomes.

Decision-Making

Because Thibaut and Kelley build their model from a drive-reduction position, their conception of decision-making is based upon reinforcement resulting from need fulfillment. They suggest that the probability a person will perform a certain behavior is a function of the internal (emotions) and external stimuli (environmental force) associated with the behavior and reinforcements previously gained from engaging in the behavior. Thus, behavior that should maximize outcomes is chosen.

However, they note limitations to this model. A person might engage in a behavior which is not associated with positive outcomes if the behavior is so automatic that it occurs with little cognitive control. They note that some communication behaviors are so ritualized that they may be engaged in without thinking. Because we have been socialized to use the pronoun "he" when describing a human, it may be used without much awareness and control. While this response may be generally rewarded or at least ignored, a feminist probably will not reinforce it. Still, it is difficult to alter language despite negative reinforcements because of the years of socialization during which it was acceptable.

Another limitation of their analysis of decision-making stems from novel situations. In initial encounters, we may have little basis to determine what the most rewarding behavior is likely to be, and, therefore, our behavior may be unrewarded. However, Thibaut and Kelley argue that people learn to respond in a reinforced way and soon adapt to the limitations.

However, one of the most interesting parts of their theory stems not from predicting behavior but from analyzing one's evaluation of a relationship. The evaluation of a relationship involves comparing one's outcomes from a relationship with two standards: comparison level and comparison level for alternatives. Comparison level represents what a person feels should be received in the way of rewards and costs from a relationship. It

Relationship 1:	O	>	CL	>	CL_{alt} =	Satisfying and Stable
Relationship 2:	O	>	CL_{alt}	>	CL =	Satisfying and Stable
Relationship 3:	CL	>	O	>	CL_{alt} =	Unsatisfying and Stable
Relationship 4:	CL	>	CL_{alt}	>	O =	Unsatisfying and Unstable
Relationship 5:	CL_{alt}	>	CL	>	O =	Unsatisfying and Unstable
Relationship 6:	CL_{alt}	>	O	>	CL =	Satisfying and Unstable

O	=	Outcomes
CL	=	Comparison Level
CL_{alt}	=	Comparison Level for Alternatives
>	=	Greater Than

FIGURE 2   The Relationship Between Outcomes, Comparison Level, and Comparison Level for Alternatives and Satisfaction and Stability

may represent the level of relational rewards received from previous relationships or from what one learns from others about the level of rewards received by others from similar relationships. The comparison between outcomes received from a current relationship and comparison level determines the person's attraction to or satisfaction with the relationship. Comparison level for alternatives represents the lowest level of relational rewards a person is willing to accept given available rewards from alternative relationships or being alone. By comparing relational outcomes with comparison level for alternatives, we get some notion of how stable the relationship is.

By comparing the relative size of relational outcomes with the two comparison levels, we should be able to predict how satisfying and stable the relationship is. Figure 2 contains the six possible combinations of outcomes and comparison levels. In *relationship 1*, outcomes are greater than comparison level. The person is satisfied because there are more rewards than expected. The person's comparison level is greater than the comparison level for alternatives, making the relationship stable. To some degree, the person is highly dependent upon the relationship. The individual is getting more than expected but should the relationship fail (e.g., through death of the partner), alternative sources of rewards are less than are expected from relationships.

Relationship 2 is quite similar to the one described above. The person is satisfied with the relationship because the outcomes are greater than comparison level, and the relationship is stable because the outcomes are greater than the comparison level for alternatives. However, the person in this relationship is not quite as dependent upon the relationship, since alternative relationships offer greater rewards than expected. If this relationship is ended then others will still be acceptable.

Relationship 3 represents relational trouble. The person's expectations about relational rewards (comparison level) is higher than outcomes from the current relationship and rewards from other relationships. The person is dissatisfied with this relationship but the relationship is likely to be stable because the person perceives outcomes are better than those from alternative relationships. The person is trapped in an unsatisfactory relationship. Such a relationship is termed nonvoluntary.

Relationship 4 involves a person who is dissatisfied with relational rewards because outcomes from the relationship are lower than expected. However, the person is not trapped since the comparison level for alternatives is greater than outcomes. The person would be likely to form a new relationship or choose to be alone since these alternatives offer greater rewards than those in the current unsatisfactory relationship. I would not be overly optimistic about this person's new relationship, though. Because this person has such high ideals, even the new alternative will be unsatisfactory. The person is likely to be constantly dissatisfied.

Relationships 5 and 6 may be tantamount to no relationship. In each case, the person's anticipated rewards from alternatives is greater than current outcomes and expected outcomes for a relationship. However, an important difference between the two should be noted. In relationship 5, the person is also dissatisfied with the relationship since outcomes are lower than comparison level. In such a case, the person dislikes the amount of rewards being received and has better alternatives. However, relationship 6 suggests that the person is satisfied with relational outcomes because they are greater than expected. Because the person could get greater rewards through alternatives, the relationship is unstable and endangered. One can be sympathetic with the person who is providing another with more rewards than expected but for some reason cannot compete with alternatives.

Exchange Patterns

Thibaut and Kelley are interested in more than individual decision-making. They are also interested in how people adjust their behaviors to each other's responses. When people are interacting, they are assumed to be enacting behavioral sequences. The *behavioral sequence* is a series of verbal or motor actions designed to achieve some goal. A behavioral *set* is the person's intention to achieve the goal.

Social exchange can be conceptualized as an expanded version of a game matrix. Unlike the two-person matrix described earlier, two exchange partners can often choose between more than just two behaviors.

During an evening, a couple might choose to watch television, go to a movie, go to a restaurant, go to bed, or play backgammon. Like the two-person matrix, the outcomes of performing a given behavior are also influenced by the behavior of the other person. If one person says, "I am going to play backgammon," and the other says, "I am going to watch TV," the outcomes for each might be expected to be different than if they both chose the same outcomes. Since backgammon, unlike TV viewing, normally requires two people, different choices may result in losses for the person who desires to play the game. Thus, the rewards associated with the choice of a behavior are partly determined by exogenous factors (e.g., the skill of the couple when playing backgammon) and endogenous factors (e.g., whether the other person is willing to play backgammon rather than watch TV).

Given that one's outcomes are partly dependent upon the behavior of others, relational partners will be concerned about their relative ability to influence each other's behavior or to exert power over them. According to Thibaut and Kelley, power is based upon the dependence a person has on another for outcomes. The greater the dependence of person A on person B for rewards, the greater the power of person B over person A. Power takes two forms in their model: fate control and behavior control. *Fate control* is the ability to affect another's outcomes regardless of what that person does. If one person is highly dependent upon another for a resource such as love, then the other can affect the person's outcomes by simply refusing to give love regardless of what the person does. With no available sources of love, the person is under the partner's control. *Behavior control* involves the ability to cause variations in another's behavior by varying one's own behavior. Fate control assumes that by withholding or providing a behavior regardless of the other's behavior, one gains power. Behavior control suggests that one can influence another by choosing alternative behaviors that are rewarding to another only if the other chooses a given alternative. If one person in a dyad decides to read a book, then that increases the likelihood that the other will choose to engage in some behavior which can be done alone. Since reading is generally a solitary action, the other person will not find an action which requires two people very rewarding.

Since unilateral power can lead to exploitation, people are interested in protecting themselves from abuse. To that end, people develop power strategies to deal with inequities. A less powerful person may increase power by seeking alternative sources of rewards, reducing the other person's alternative sources of rewards, improving one's own ability to provide rewards, reducing the other's ability to provide rewards, persuading the other as to the value of one's own resources, or devaluing the other person's resources for self.

Because the exercise of power is often costly to individuals, norms or behavioral rules emerge. These rules specify how individuals might trade resources, coordinate their behavioral responses, or eliminate costly responses. They may develop consciously in a dyadic exchange, emerge with little awareness through trial and error, or be imposed by the larger social group. Their value stems from the certainty and predictability they provide the exchange at the relatively low cost of negotiation.

The recent works by Kelley and Thibaut (1978) and Kelley (1979) are ambitious attempts to describe the emerging patterns of exchange. As in their earlier work, they assume that social exchange can be thought of as involving a matrix containing a number of behavioral alternatives associated with rewards. However, they assert that three types of matrices exist in social exchange. The first is the *given matrix* and represents the behavioral choices and outcomes that are mandated by environmental and institutional factors in combination with internal factors such as skill. When two people are involved in an exchange, the environment may impinge upon their alternatives by making certain options very difficult to engage in (e.g., scarcity of money restricts a variety of alternatives). At the same time, two people may be deficient at performing certain behaviors, thereby making the successful completion of the behaviors very unlikely. Actually changing the given matrix is very difficult and involves changing the people or the environment.

However, people are not altogether trapped by the environmental restrictions on their exchanges. People are capable of treating the given outcomes and alternatives in ways that transform them into something different. If two people find themselves in an exchange in which neither has an action with desirable outcomes or they are uncertain as to how to choose between alternatives, they may transform their given alternatives and outcomes into what is termed the effective matrix. The effective matrix represents an expansion of alternative behaviors and/or outcomes which ultimately determines the behavioral choices in social exchange. The transformations of the given matrix result from taking into consideration one's own outcomes as well as the outcomes of the other. They may take the form of treating the given outcomes as though they were different than what they really are. For example, a husband concerned about his wife's welfare may charge himself for her services as a housewife. In this case, her outcomes are treated by him as though they were his own.

Another transformation might involve transposing who acts first in the interaction. In some cases, the person who gives a resource first may have an advantage over the person who goes next. Therefore, that response becomes more valuable than what is suggested by the given matrix. Finally, two people might transform the given matrix by considering their previous history of exchanges and formulate a future policy of matching or not matching the partner's exchanges. In any case, the transformation represents a rule by which two people alter their conceptions of their alternative behaviors and the associated outcomes in an interaction. It is a strategy which guides their behavior in the exchange.

The final matrix is the dispositional matrix and represents the orientations that two people have about how rewards ought to be exchanged. The orientations partly guide the transformations used to create the effective matrix. For example, some people have Machiavellian attitudes (Christie and Geis, 1970). Such individuals have values that suggest that winning is important. As such, they are predisposed to view exchanges as competition (see Rubin and Brown, 1975). When looking at the given alternatives and outcomes, we might expect a high Machiavellian to figure a way of transforming the alternatives and outcomes in such a way so as to maximize personal rewards relative to another's. Thus, if we know the kinds of dispositions a person has, we should be able to predict the strategy which might be used in the interaction with us. We could adopt appropriate counterstrategies to prevent exploitation.

The dispositional matrix is not the sole determinant of transformations; the nature of the situation (given matrix) may also influence the transformation. There may be some situations that are so imbalanced that even a high Machiavellian would not need to transform them. In addition, the dispositional matrix may also be influenced by the actual outcomes in the given matrix. Even a high Machiavellian may become disgruntled if success is found in gaining greater rewards than others but the absolute value of the rewards are found to be insufficient for personal needs.

Thibaut and Kelley provide us with the most complete and complex notion of exchange patterns. Their terminology is novel and their application of gaming principles extensive.

FOA AND FOA'S RESOURCE THEORY

Foa and Foa are also social psychologists. They have written a variety of articles (Foa, 1971; Foa and Foa, 1972; Foa and Foa, 1976) and one book (Foa and Foa, 1974), *Societal Structures of the Mind*, in which they explicate their theory.

Underlying Theoretical Base

Unlike the other Social Exchange Theories we have examined, Resource Theory does not really arise from a single theoretical base. Foa and Foa are building an approach which attempts to integrate a variety of theories in psychology. Their perspective seeks to reconcile the effects of reinforcement with cognitive structures which influence behavior. In order to achieve this lofty goal, they focus on cognitive structures or the conceptual categories that organize events and stimuli. Cognitive structures develop from processes of differentiation and generalization. Differentiation means that objects are perceived as distinct; generalization means that common attributes are distinguished.

Importantly, Foa and Foa see cognitive structures as developing over time. Cognitive categories are not present at birth and some develop before others. Their analysis of this development process is quite interesting. Foa and Foa suggest that at birth, a newborn's environment is undifferentiated. The baby receives love and services from parents but is unable to distinguish between the two resources. After the infant learns to do things (e.g., dress and eat), differences between love and instrumental services are perceived. At about the same time, the child begins to perceive the difference between self and others. Behaviorally, the infant also learns the difference between giving and taking (or denying) a resource.

Later the child learns to distinguish between actual and ideal behaviors. The child wishes to engage in a given activity but is denied the opportunity. Behaviorally, the child comes to understand the difference between being an object of a behavior rather than the source of a behavior. About this time, the child learns to distinguish status from love and goods from services. A child discovers that praise or blame for a behavior can be received without it necessarily being related to being loved. In addition, the child may discover that some goods like food disappear whereas the service of cooking appears repeatedly.

Finally, the individual learns that the viewpoint of an actor and observer are often different. Parents are often horrified by a child's tendency to eat undesirable objects such as dirt. Children soon learn that their views differ from parents' views. At this stage, the child learns to differentiate information from status and money from goods. The child learns that reading or remembering certain facts is often reinforced through praise. Thus, information is a commodity that is often associated with a gain in status. Similarly, the child learns about money with the discovery that it is often necessary to exchange money for goods such as candy or toys.

Thus, an adult has a variety of cognitive structures about interpersonal exchanges that allow the development of meaning for the events that occur in an exchange. A person understands the difference between self and others, giving and taking, and resource types. As is implied by the name of their theory, the resources are the focus of their approach. They examine six resource categories: love, services, status, information, goods, and money, which differ on how particularistic or universalistic and concrete or abstract they are. The remaining portion of their theory focuses on the variables that guide the exchanges of these resources.

Decision-Making

Behavior is guided by motivational states, and people are motivated to engage in certain behaviors whenever quantities of resources fall outside the optimal range. The optimal range represents the points between a lower amount of a resource below which the person feels a need for that resource and will be motivated to gain more of it, and an upper amount beyond which a person feels satiated and is motivated to exchange some of that resource for some other. Optimum range varies from resource to resource. Love is thought to have a narrow optimum range. Service and status have wider optimum ranges than love but less than goods and information. Money is thought to have the widest optimum range, with an upper bound moving toward infinity.

When a person has greater resources than the lower bound of the optimal range, then that person can conceivably afford to enter into an exchange for another resource. Potentially that person has a great deal of power because of the possession of an amount of a resource greater than the least amount needed. However, actual power requires that others need or desire the person's resource. If one possesses a great ability to provide services but that service is not in demand, then one is left powerless in exchange.

Thus, the basic mechanism for stimulating the choice of a behavior is the need to acquire or relinquish a resource.

Exchange Patterns

Foa and Foa are concerned with specifying the rules that guide the exchange of resources. They (1976: 106) posit two propositions: "(1) Every interpersonal behavior consists of giving and/or taking away one or more resources; and (2) Behaviors that involve closely allied resources occur more frequently than behaviors that involve less closely related resources."

Of the two propositions, the second one is more important for predicting how resources will be exchanged. The theory assumes that a given resource tends to be seen as more or less similar to other resources. Love is similar to status and services, somewhat different than goods and information, and very different from money. In fact, love, services, and status are so similar that they may be transferred together in the same behavior.

Research (see, Foa and Foa, 1974, 1976) largely supports their position. Questionnaire responses indicate a tendency to exchange rewards in kind; e.g., love for love, money for money. This tendency is strongest for particularistic resources such as love, status, and services, and less so for universalistic resources such as goods and money. While information is universalistic, it tended to be exchanged in kind as well. Their similarity prediction also holds true. If one does not receive the same resource given, the preference is for receiving a similar one; e.g., goods for money, status for love. Questionnaire responses have also indicated that the form of the exchange relationship influences the exchange of resources. Friendship relationships most likely involve exchanges of love, status, information, and services rather than goods and money. When examining relationships of an undefined nature, the exchange of money and goods increased dramatically.

When examining actual exchanges rather than hypothetical ones, the theory also receives support. An experimental situation was constructed in which subjects gave one resource but received in return either money or expressions of love. As predicted, satisfaction with the exchange was lower when the exchange involved dissimilar rewards.

Denial of a resource has also been studied. It was expected, and confirmed that people would attempt to deny resources similar to the ones initially taken away. While denial of love appeared to be a universal weapon for retaliation, a general tendency to retaliate in kind was found. When examining actual exchanges, the denial of a similar resource to that taken away was observed. Interestingly, when a person is forced to retaliate with a highly dissimilar resource (e.g., money for love), the person tends to increase the intensity of the denial. This result seems to indicate that adequate compensation for the loss requires increased amounts of a dissimilar resource. Thus, a spurned lover can adequately restore equity by denying a "friend" love. If infatuation is so strong that such a denial is impossible, then the person will deny a dissimilar resource, and lots of it. However, one of my students developed an interesting variation on this finding. He suggested that a better way to get even for a denial of love is to go to your former lover and say, "Gee, I feel badly that we have parted ways abruptly. I haven't had the opportunity to repay you for all the love and satisfaction you have given me during our relationship. Here is a quarter!"

Thus, one might compensate for the use of a dissimilar resource in retaliation by increasing the intensity of its denial. However, research indicates that even when the intensity is increased the person is still frustrated.

Foa and Foa have provided us with an explanation of the resources of exchange and have attempted to describe how they are exchanged. Their research tends to support their conceptualization.

WALSTER, BERSCHEID, AND WALSTER'S EQUITY THEORY

Equity Theories have generated a great deal of empirical research. Indeed, over 400 studies from a variety of disciplines have been catalogued by Walster et al. (1978). The primary sources for their Equity Theory are found in an article (Walster, Berscheid, and Walster, 1976) and a book (Walster, Walster, and Berscheid, 1978), *Equity: Theory and Research.*

Underlying Theoretical Base

Equity Theory is meant to be more than just one of the Social Exchange Theories. Like Foa and Foa, Walster et al. seek to create a theory that will integrate a variety of psychological theories. Indeed, they hope to avoid the trap of creating a mini-theory and seek a general theory of social interaction.

The underlying theoretical base comes from the work of the other Social Exchange Theorists. As noted earlier, Homans (1961) and Blau (1964b) have explored the concept of distributive justice. Briefly, distributive justice describes the reactions of a person whose outcomes are less desirable than a person with similar investments.

Adams (1965) developed distributive justice into an early version of Equity Theory in which equity is defined as the perception that one's ratio of outcomes to inputs (roughly rewards to costs) is equal to the ratio of outcomes to inputs of some other person with whom one has an exchange relationship, some other person who is also having an exchange with one's exchange partner, or some other person who is in a comparable exchange relationship with a different person. If the two ratios are unequal, then inequity is said to exist and the people feel an unpleasant emotional state. A person suffering an inequity might alter inputs or outcomes, cognitively distort inputs and outputs, leave the exchange, change perceptions of another's inputs and outputs, or find a new comparison person in order to reestablish equity. Adams' framework has generated a great deal of research (see Adams and Freedman, 1976, for a review) and provided a source of stimulation for Walster et al.

Decision-Making

Walster et al. have created specific propositions. At the heart of their theory is the notion that people are selfish and will act according to their self-interests. This notion is reflected in their first proposition: "Individuals will try to maximize their outcomes (where outcomes equal rewards minus costs)" (Walster et al., 1976: 6). Thus, people seek maximization of profits, echoing other Social Exchange Theories.

But, their corollary adds a somewhat different twist: "So long as individuals perceive they can maximize their outcomes by behaving equitably, they will do so. Should they perceive that they can maximize their outcomes by behaving inequitably they will do so." (Walster et al., 1976: 16). People adjust their behaviors to provide the greatest outcomes regardless of the impact upon others. If a situation demands fairness in order to obtain profit, they will act accordingly; if, however, getting ahead requires exploitation, they will also act accordingly.

At this juncture, it is important to examine their definition of equity. An equitable relationship is one in which some person (a participant in the exchange or outside observer) perceives that the relative gains of two people in an exchange are equal. The relative gains imply that a comparison is made between two ratios representing the net gain of each person in the exchange. The ratio for each person is defined by the difference between outcomes and inputs divided by the absolute value of inputs. By comparing the two ratios, we should obtain some notion of how equitable the distribution of profit is in the relationship, at least as seen by an individual scrutinizing the relationship.

Exchange Patterns

At this point, Equity Theory assumes flexibility in achieving the best profit. However, the best way to achieve profit is often influenced by other people and the remaining propositions delineate how people reach decisions.

One source of influence on the person's decision to be equitable or inequitable is society. In proposition IIA, Walster et al. (1976: 6) state: "Groups can maximize collective rewards by evolving accepted systems for equitably apportioning resources among members. Thus, groups will evolve such a system of equity and will attempt to induce members to accept and adhere to these systems." Proposition IIB reads: "Groups will generally punish (increase the costs for) members who treat others inequitably" (Walster et al., 1976: 6). People have discovered that their society will be more stable if the self-interests of individuals can be mutually provided rather than through unilateral attainment of goals. Therefore, society has created norms and formal laws to insure that some equity is established in exchange relationships. Certainly, divorce laws might be thought of as attempts to insure that the property and goods of a relationship are equitably distributed.

Because of the potential for societal retribution and the threat of retaliation by a relational partner, people have come to respond with distress when an inequity arises and, consequently, they seek to restore equity. Proposition III states: "When individuals find themselves participating in inequitable relationships, they become distressed. The more inequitable the relationship the more distressed the individual will feel." Proposition IV describes the response to being distressed: "Individuals who discover they are in an inequitable relationship attempt to eliminate their distress by restoring equity. The greater the inequity that exists, the more distress they feel and the harder they try to restore equity" (Walster et al., 1976: 6).

While inequity and exploitation may arise in some relationships, Equity Theory predicts that it may be short-lived. Society and relational partners are motivated to restore equity through some means. In Chapter 4 of this book, we will explore how these equity-restoring desires might be related to interpersonal conflict, but for now it should suffice to know that something will be done to restore equity.

In summary, we have explored the underlying theoretical base, the description of decision-making, and the exchange patterns of five Social Exchange Theories. Homans moves from the principles of operant psychology and advances propositions which should explain interpersonal social exchange. Blau focuses on emergent properties of the exchange and applies principles derived from economics. Thibaut and Kelley examine how people evaluate outcomes from a relationship and how outcomes arise from their interdependence. They suggest that people can transform their alternatives and outcomes into a strategy consistent with their dispositions. Foa and Foa describe the developmental process leading to exchange and explore the rules which guide the exchange of resources. Finally, Walster, Berscheid, and Walster focus on how rewards are distributed in relationships. People are motivated to seek profit in a relationship because of societal standards and the concerns of their relational partners, and also become concerned with the equitable distribution of profits.

NOTES

1. The following is a list of the major critiques: Turner, 1961; Boulding, 1962; Davis, 1962; Deutsch, 1964; Deutsch and Krauss, 1965; Abrahamsson, 1970; Maris, 1970; Blain, 1971a, b; Mulkay, 1971; Simpson, 1972; Ekeh, 1974; Turner, 1974; Skidmore, 1975; Chadwick-Jones, 1976; Emerson, 1976; Heath, 1976; Gergen, 1977; Gibbs, 1977; Johnson, 1977; Bredemerier, 1978; Mitchell, 1978; Skidmore, 1979.

2. It should be noted Homans does discuss the implications of economics and gaming principles for his theory. But his theory is primarily based upon principles of operant psychology.

3. Two points should be noted initially. First, Kelley and Thibaut (1978) and Kelley (1979) have indicated that they consider their theory to be more than just an exchange perspective. It also deals with issues such as coordination. My discussion of their approach will focus on aspects of their theory related to exchange. Second, the title, "Theory of Interdependence" stems from their most recent writings. I have subsumed material published prior to their current thinking into this theory as well.

3

RELATIONAL DEVELOPMENT

A central area of theory and research in interpersonal communication concerns factors related to the development of interpersonal relationships. The study of relational development has focused on variables that stimulate interpersonal attraction, informational changes that accompany relational development, and communication processes that impede or facilitate changes in a relationship. This chapter applies each of the five Social Exchange Theories to these factors.

> *We cannot tell the precise moment when friendship is formed. As in filling a vessel drop by drop, there is at last a drop which makes it run over; so in a series of kindnesses there is at last one which makes the heart run over.*
>
> James Boswell
> 1791

While almost two centuries old, the above quotation suggests several points about relational development that communication scholars have come to accept. First, it implies that relationships are formed rather than innate. Even though some relationships, such as those between relatives, are determined by cultural ascriptions, the exact nature of the relationship develops over time. Indeed, variations in parent/child relationships can be observed within the same culture. Second, the quotation implies that the developmental process is gradual rather than immediate. Although some relationships may develop quickly due to "love at first sight," relational partners must still learn to coordinate their activities over time. Finally, the quotation suggests that relational changes are associated with exchanges between people. Relational partners provide each other with objects or activities that prompt changes in the nature of the relationship as the exchanges continue.

In fact, each of these points represents a rich research area. Scholars have investigated the factors that influence interpersonal attraction (see, Murstein, 1971a, Huston, 1974; Clore, 1976; Duck, 1977; and Berscheid and Walster, 1978, for extensive review of this literature). Miller and Steinberg (1975) have extended this analysis into the conditions that prompt relational partners to escalate or change their relationships. They suggest that three conditions stimulate relational change. First, people tend to be susceptible to relational escalation at times of relational scarcity (too few relationships for our needs), personal crisis, or self-concept development. Second, relational change is often caused by the desire of the relational partners to form a closer relationship. The escalation is created intentionally. Finally, relational change is stimulated by the perception that one can gain relational profit from escalation. People expect to get more from the relationship than they have to put into it.

Researchers have studied changes that take place in the gradual process of relational development. Different patterns emerge as the relationship develops. Of particular importance are the changes in the information the relational partners have about each other. Elsewhere (Roloff, 1976), I have suggested that relational change involves increases or decreases in the ability of relational parties to use certain kinds of information to make predictions about each other. As relationships escalate, the partners are better able to make predictions about each other because they have more access to private information about one another. As a relationship deescalates, the predictions become less accurate as the partners rely upon stereotypic information. Escalation should be related to greater understanding of the partner, whereas deescalation should be related to less understanding of the partner.

Finally, communication researchers have focused on the role of communication processes in stimulating these changes. Because of our intrinsic need to predict and explain another's behavior, Berger and Calabrese (1975) predict that certain communication behaviors should be observed in developing relationships. Verbal communication (particularly self-disclosing messages) and nonverbal affiliative behaviors (e.g., eye contact, voice quality) should reduce uncertainty about another person's behaviors. They provide information about one's previous behavior and indicate how one views the emotional nature of the relationship. Since these communication behaviors tend to be reciprocated by relational partners, we might expect that a person wishing to escalate a relationship might use them as stimuli to learn more about the other. If one self-discloses to another then the other will likely self-disclose in return, thereby allowing both to increase their understanding of each other.

Given the importance of relational development, it is necessary that we examine what the Social Exchange Theories have to say about it. We will examine how each of the five theories would characterize interpersonal attraction, indicators of relational change, and self-disclosing communication.

HOMANS' OPERANT PSYCHOLOGY APPROACH

Since Homans built this theory upon the principles of operant psychology, relational development is a function of previous reinforcement schedules. His propositions should account for such relational changes.

Interpersonal Attraction

While Homans' book did not specifically address the issue of interpersonal attraction, he did write an article discussing power and interpersonal attraction (Homans, 1971a). He suggested that interpersonal attraction consists of two parts. On one hand, it is the liking or admiration one person feels for another. It is a positive evaluative or emotional response to another. On the other hand, interpersonal attraction is a person's willingness to approach, be near and/or interact with another. While the first component of attraction is a covert emotional response, the second part is more behavioral and observable. Further, the two parts are not necessarily related. A person may have positive emotional or evaluative response to another but not communicate with the person.

A person's attraction to another is simply a response to a stimulus. The likelihood that the response will be repeated is a function of the consequences the response creates. To the extent that the attraction results in the attainment of positively valued resources (rewards), it is reinforced and is more likely to be emitted in similar situations in the future. Thus, if a person wanted to attract another, the person should reward the other's emotional or behavioral responses.

However, creating attraction may be problematic. If one is interested in creating attraction as defined by a positive emotional or evaluative response, then one must reinforce that response when it occurs. A person may be faced with the difficulty of creating the response initially. In other words, the response must occur at least once before it may be reinforced. A person may have to wait for the response to occur naturally and then reinforce it.

An additional difficulty stems from determining when the response has occurred. How do we know when the person is experiencing the positive evaluative or emotional response? Some have argued that our emotional responses and facial affect displays are so closely linked that they are, under certain circumstances, the same (see Ekman, Friesen, and Ellsworth 1971). A person who is happy automatically smiles. Therefore, one could reinforce positive affect displays made in one's presence in order to increase the likelihood that the other would become more attracted. However, Ekman, Friesen, and Ellsworth note that people have an ability to control their facial affect through display rules, and high self-monitors are particularly adept at controlling their affect displays so that what is seen is not always what is being felt (Snyder, 1974, 1979). Consequently, a person may accidentally reinforce affect that is unrelated to attraction.

Similarly, one must reinforce another's behaviors in order to create attraction based upon the willingness to be with, near, or interacting with oneself. A person must decide what behavioral form of attraction to reinforce. Is talking sufficient, or must other nonverbal affiliative behaviors also be present (e.g., touching, eye contact)? After determining the appropriate target behavior, one must wait for its natural occurrence. After reinforcing the behavioral attraction, one should find it frequently occurring in similar situations in the future.

Regardless of whether one is concerned with creating emotional or behavioral attraction, a person must also determine the appropriate reward to be used as a reinforcer. Research indicates that a variety of social rewards might be used to reinforce another's attraction. The most obvious reinforcer is expressing attraction for the other. As noted by Berscheid and Walster (1978: 59), "Psychologists consistently find that people like people whom they think like them." When the target person smiles, smile back. When the target person begins to interact with you, be responsive. Indeed, even minimal signs of approval in a conversation tends to increase a variety of communication behaviors (see, Gergen, 1969: 19-33 for a closer review of this literature). Verplanck (1955) found that verbal approval (e.g., "You're right") and nonverbal agreement (e.g., head nodding and smiles) tended to increase the frequency of statements of opinions by another, whereas the absence of such reinforcement decreased the frequency of opinion statements. Matarazzo et al. (1964) discovered that increasing head nods during a conversation tended to increase the duration of a source's statements, whereas decreasing amounts of head nodding resulted in less talking.

It should be noted that too consistent a response of attraction for attraction can backfire. As noted in Homans' deprivation-satiation proposition, the more of a reward we have received in the recent past, the less valuable any further unit of that reward becomes. Thus, a person who frequently receives positive affective responses from another may become satiated with them, and the reinforcer becomes less effective in creating attraction. Gerwirtz and Baer (1958) observed that the effectiveness of verbal approval is affected by a person's deprivation levels. Consistent with Homans' satiation-deprivation proposition, children who had been deprived of social approval immediately prior to a task were more responsive to statements of social approval (e.g., "good," "fine") during the task than children who had been satiated or at least not deprived of social approval prior to the task. Thus, the receiver has some control over a source's communication behaviors and behavioral attraction.

Social approval might also be used to reinforce emotional attraction. Research by Clore and McGuire (1974) demonstrated that the more positive statements made in a conversation, the more liking, and the more negative statements, the less liking. However, the relationship between approval and liking is very complex (see Mettee and Aronson, 1974). Only under certain circumstances do we find stated approval of another being related to liking of the communicator and, in some cases, initial disapproval followed by approval leads to greater attraction than consistently stated approval (see Aronson and Linder, 1965). While this latter finding is also qualified by a variety of necessary conditions for it to exist, it does suggest that consistent approval leads to less attraction than approval that is provided less frequently. We might argue that consistently stated approval loses its value due to satiation. Just as we pointed out before, a person may come to like us more if we vary our reinforcement for that emotion than if we consistently provide a single reward such as social approval. While research has found that people who consistently disapprove of us or initially state their approval and then deny it are disliked, we might find that over a series of interactions (at least more than two) individuals will be attracted to others who extend their approval on a variable basis rather than with a consistent pattern. Even if initial positive statements are followed by negative ones in a second interaction, the occurrence of positive evaluations in later interactions may lead to higher attraction than consistently positive evaluation throughout all the interactions.

Homans (1971a) argues that interpersonal attraction may be a function of power. He explores several definitions of power but seems to arrive at two that are related to attraction. The first type of power stems from what Waller and Hill (1951: 191) referred to as the principle of least interest. This principle states, "That person is able to dictate the conditions of association whose interest in the continuation of the affair is the least." Thus, a person is more powerful than another when having less interest (receiving less profit) in rewarding the relational partner than the relational partner has in rewarding him, and the more interested partner changes behavior to reward the less interested person. In such cases, the attraction of the less powerful person may stem from an attempt to keep the more powerful person interested in the relationship. It is a way of equalizing the exchange by providing an additional source of reward. Since such relationships can often lead to the exploitation of the less powerful person, Homans notes that the two parts of attraction may be separated. The greater dependence of the weaker person may mandate a continuing of behavioral attraction to the more powerful person but the emotional attraction to the individual will no longer be felt. Homans suggests a more equal distribution of power is more likely to lead to increased emotional and behavioral attraction on the part of both individuals for each other.

The second form of power comes from knowledge of how to attain rewards. This form of power generally leads to emotional attraction as the information recipient becomes grateful for advice leading to reward attainment. However, Homans does not believe that this form of power always leads to behavioral attraction. A person may perceive that the advice will not produce rewards commensurate with the costs of obtaining them. A recent divorcee may be grateful for the well-intended advice of friends but wish to avoid contact and communication if the costs of carrying out the advice are too great. Indeed, talking with the friends may be costly since the friends may inquire as to why the person has not yet carried out their advice.

Thus, interpersonal attraction is a function of the rewards one has received for being attracted to another. The ability to provide rewards may be dependent upon a person's power.

Indicators of Relational Change

While communication scholars have focused on changes in information as an indicant of relational change, Homans focuses on expansion of exchange as a key indicator of relational development. People become attracted to each other based on the rewards they receive for their attraction. The more rewards they receive for their emotional or behavioral attraction, the more likely they are to repeat those responses in the future. As people consistently reward one another in one area of exchange, Homans suggests that they have a tendency to expand their exchange into other areas.

Homans uses Heider's Balance Model (1958) to describe this expansion. Several examples would be useful. As a result of previously rewarding exchanges, people come to like each other. This positive affection often leads them to interact more often with each other. In the process of interaction, they may come to learn that they agree or disagree about certain other objects. If two people like one another, and in the process of interacting discover that they both like the same things, then their relationship is balanced. Homans argues that this newfound agreement is, in and of itself, rewarding and represents an expansion of the exchange into the area of attitudes. Although not cited by Homans, Byrne and his associates (Byrne, 1971; Clore and Byrne, 1974) have demonstrated that attitudinal similarity operates as a reward because it provides consensual validation for one's position.

However, if two people who like each other discover that they disagree about some third object or person, the relationship is unbalanced. In such cases, the exchange relationship may be threatened. Indeed, one of the parties may change an attitude to conform to the other person's *or* may simply invalidate the previous history of exchanges and refuse to engage in further exchanges, unless the other person changes.

Thus, for a relationship to expand, some balance must be achieved with regard to other exchange areas. If two people reach agreement in other areas, the relationship persists or even expands further. If no agreement is reached, the relationship will dwindle as the partners cease exchanging with one another.

As the number of exchanges expand, the nature of the relationship changes from an impersonal one to a personal one. An *impersonal relationship* is one in which two people exchange a single reward with each other and the reward is readily available from a large number of suppliers. In such a relationship, the exchange is not based upon principles of balance but upon the value of the reward being exchanged. *Personal relationships* are those in which two people frequently exchange rewards that are relatively scarce (relatively few suppliers). Homans argues that personal relationships are guided by the history of exchange between two people rather than the value of a single reward. Indeed, personal relationships operate according to the balance principle as the number of exchanges expand into other areas.

Leik and Leik (1977) have expanded upon Homans' thinking by suggesting that relational changes can be described as stages. The first stage is one of no commitments to exchange partners. In this stage, the person is actively seeking an exchange partner possibly because of the end of an exchange relationship. The second stage is called strict exchange. In this stage, two people have agreed to provide benefits to each other. However, their agreement is simply a "business only" deal. They expect to have reciprocal exchanges and that each will provide resources on time. If a person does not reciprocate the rewards received then the exchange ends. The relational partners are always monitoring their environment for a better exchange agreement. Therefore, strict exchange is more likely to dissolve than expand. The third stage is called confidence. In this stage, exchange partners may accept short term losses as long as the belief remains that they will be compensated for in the future. The person monitors alternative sources of rewards but compares them with projected long-term rewards of the existing relationship rather than current outcomes. However, a relationship at the confidence stage is more likely to revert back to strict exchange rather than expand to the fourth stage. The fourth stage is called interpersonal commitment and is a stage in which two people do not consider alternative sources of rewards. The two people are totally absorbed by their exchange relationship and are not even considering other sources of rewards.

Given this definition of commitment, one would expect that relationships that reach this level would never voluntarily end. However, Leik and Leik recognize that relationships do end and they suggest a phenomenon which may account for these events: people have different relationships dealing with different aspects of their lives. Some people have romantic relationships, work relationships, and friendship relationships that are often separate from one another. If a person is at the commitment stage in a romantic relationship, then a change in the stage of another relationship may threaten the commitment to the romantic relationship. For example, an increased commitment to a friendship may challenge the commitment to the romantic relationship since similar rewards are provided by the two.

Thus, relational development may involve stages in which a person becomes committed to the exchange partner as the relational partners expand their exchange areas.

Self-Disclosing Communication

While Homans does not specifically deal with self-disclosure, his work is often cited as a theoretical base for research on self-disclosure. It may seem odd for a dedicated behaviorist such as Homans to be concerned with a concept containing the term "self." The act of disclosing about self implies that a person has been monitoring personal behavior and thinking. However, if one returns to the analysis provided by Skinner (1974) it is possible to infer how Homans might define self-disclosure. Skinner suggests that people are often sufficiently self-aware and able to report information about their previous reinforcement histories. Since this history may only be known by the individual, it closely resembles what most scholars would consider self-disclosing communication. Therefore, self-disclosure might be considered a description of one's personal reinforcement schedule, and since self-disclosure is simply another form of behavior, we expect it to be influenced by principles of operant conditioning. In other words, a person should be expected to engage in self-disclosure to the extent to which it produces rewards. Indeed, research suggests that self-disclosure often results in the attainment of a variety of rewards. Kleinke (1979) has reviewed research which indicates that moderate and high self-disclosure tends to result in liking for the source, and prompts self-disclosure from the listener. Thus, a person who self-discloses to another and receives affection or self-disclosure in return may be very likely to engage in more self-disclosure in the future.

However, if the person does not receive rewards but instead receives punishment, then the behavior will not be repeated. Indeed, Miller and Steinberg (1975) have suggested that self-disclosure is risky since the receiver might reject the source based upon disclosure of negative information or might use the information against the source. Research by Gilbert and Horenstein (1975) and Dalto, Ajzen, and Kaplan (cited in Ajzen, 1977) has found that disclosure of negative intimate information does not produce as much attraction as disclosure of positive information, whether it be intimate or superficial.

By providing the relational partners with more precise information about each other, self-disclosing communications are facilitators of relational development. In Homans' theory, self-disclosure may simply represent another area of exchange which expands the relationship. After exchanging in one area, the couple may expand their exchanges into self-disclosure of their reinforcement histories. If they find their self-disclosures rewarded by each other, then the relationship is balanced and further exchange continues. If the self-disclosure leads to punishment, then the exchange relationship is threatened with extinction. Thus, the information transmitted is less important than the consequence of transmitting it.

BLAU'S ECONOMIC APPROACH

Blau recognizes the importance of emergent properties and emphasizes economic principles.

Interpersonal Attraction

Blau (1964a) does not specifically define interpersonal attraction but does place a great deal of emphasis on a similar phenomenon he calls social attraction, the tendency of people to associate with each other. The concept seems to include both an emotional desire to be with others and the behavioral tendency to form exchange relationships with them.

Social attraction is a function of the rewards a person expects to receive from creating an exchange relationship with another. These expected rewards are compared with the reward potential of other people in the relational marketplace as well as the projected rewards from being alone, and the most profitable alternative is chosen. The reward potential of a person is determined by the extrinsic services or objects provided and intrinsic rewards that arise from simply being with the person (see Rubin, 1973: 79-82 for instructions on "how to be a rewarding person").

The relational marketplace is analogous to the economic marketplace, thus, we might expect that a person's attractiveness to others is influenced by supply and demand for his resources. A person who has resources that are quite common among relational competitors may not be too attractive to other relational partners unless demand outstrips the available supply. From the view of the individual, a desirable situation is one in which others have strong desires for her resource but relatively few people are available who can provide it (high demand, low supply). One of my students indicated that she had attended an engineering college which was populated primarily by males. The small number of females on campus created a high demand for female companionship. As a result, coeds found themselves in excellent bargaining positions for relational resources.

However, Blau suggests that dangers arise in relational bartering. A person must "advertise" resource potential to others but must not be too liberal in providing samples. If one provides too much of a resource too often, the demand may lessen and reward potential slackens. Thus, a person faces a dilemma: how to provide enough of a resource to create attraction but not disperse it too freely for fear of devaluation.

A final danger arises when the supply of relational partners is increased. My female student noted that on occasions when coeds from surrounding universities visited the engineering college, the supply of female companions increased and her bargaining position (at least momentarily) deteriorated.

Indicators of Relational Change

Blau believes that exchange relationships evolve slowly and move from relatively minor exchanges into more important areas as trust develops. When a person receives an initial resource from another, the receiver becomes obligated to return some resource to the giver in order to discharge the obligation. If the obligation is discharged, the original giver may respond with new resources prompting further exchange. As long as the obligations are discharged, trust gradually builds and the relationship becomes charged with emotion. We come to like those people with whom we have engaged in fair exchanges.

This pattern of exchange is similar to what Gouldner (1960: 171) refers to as the norm of reciprocity. The norm of reciprocity states that "(1) people should help those who have helped them, and (2) people should not injure those who have helped them." From Blau's point of view, the norm of reciprocity helps to reinforce the natural tendencies of exchange. It is in the self-interest of exchange partners to discharge obligations in a manner similar to the norm of reciprocity. Therefore, norms reinforce an existing tendency.

Like Homans, Blau suggests that we should find that the frequency and variety of exchanges should expand as the relationship develops. In addition, we should find feelings of obligation to the other person and trust in the other person increasing as the relationship develops.

Self-Disclosing Communication

As noted earlier, people must find a way of making others aware of their reward potential relative to other competitors. While Blau does not specifically discuss self-disclosure, his analysis implies that self-disclosure is a form of "relational advertising." Most people know more about their own distinctive characteristics (resources in low supply) that may be valuable to others than outside observers do. Therefore, it is in their self-interest to make those distinctive characteristics known to potential relational partners. In other words, a person who is seeking to attract another may self-disclose the unique and hidden characteristics that are likely to be valued by the target.

However, dangers are implicit in this disclosure. One may inaccurately predict the value of distinctive characteristics to another. The other person may reject the exchange based upon a negatively valued trait. Therefore, people tend to be cautious when self-disclosing. Blau (1964a: 39) writes, "The fear of antagonizing associates and being rejected by them is the reason individuals tend to confine themselves to subtle hints about their most distinctive traits and opinions in the initial stages of acquaintance."

In addition, self-disclosure may be threatening to others. If we provide information about our unique and valued characteristics, we may prompt feelings of inferiority in the other person, who may feel unable to engage in an equitable exchange with us. In order to overcome this danger, people often engage in self-depreciation in conjunction with self-disclosure. Self-depreciation implies that the person not only releases information about reward potential but also releases information about weaknesses in other areas. A person might admit to having graduated from a prestigious university but acknowledge problems balancing a checkbook. While revealed weaknesses make the person less of a status threat, if we dislike someone, self-depreciation can lead to further disdain.

THIBAUT AND KELLEY'S
THEORY OF INTERDEPENDENCE

Thibaut and Kelley provide the most detailed analysis of relational development. It has served as a stimulus for Altman and Taylor's Social Penetration Theory (Altman and Taylor, 1973; Morton, Alexander, and Altman, 1976) and Levinger's Incremental Social Exchange Theory (Levinger and Snoek, 1972; Levinger, 1974; and Huesmann and Levinger, 1976). These revisionist theories represent refinements and extensions of many of the concepts discussed by Thibaut and Kelley.

Interpersonal Attraction

People are attracted to individuals with whom they believe they can achieve relational rewards higher than their expectations (comparison level). This assumes that a relational partner (a) has valued resources and (b) is willing to provide those resources to us.

Thibaut and Kelley have suggested a number of characteristics which lead to attraction: (1) willingness and ability to help others gain rewards or reduce costs; (2) possession of greater abilities than their own; (3) physical proximity; (4) similarity in attitudes; (5) complementary needs, and (6) status similarity. Each of these implies that a person could provide valued resources at low costs to the receiver.

However, mere possession of resources in not sufficient to create attraction. The person must be willing to behave in such a way as to facilitate the attainment of resources. In matrix terminology, the other must make transformations of the given matrix that result in an effective matrix which results in adequate rewards. If the other person makes transformations that interfere with our own reward attainment, we should not be attracted to the individual.

In order to determine what transformations another makes, we must often engage in a limited exchange. In this exchange, each person attempts to reduce uncertainty as to how outcomes compare with those from alternative relationships and whether the outcomes are likely to be provided on a stable basis.

In these limited, low-cost exchanges, the partners communicate with each other and attribute characteristics that might influence future interactions. Thibaut and Kelley note that these initial transactions are fraught with problems. The communications are often guided by inaccurate information garnered from stereotypes. Further, people who initially have positive interactions with another will expect positive outcomes in the future. These expectations are often self-fulfilling in that they produce immediate positive outcomes which are not representative of a typical mixture of positive and negative outcomes. Of course, the process might work in the opposite direction, with initially bad interactions leading to the expectation of costly outcomes. In either case, the projection of outcomes is biased.

Thus, attraction is based upon some sampling of outcomes from an exchange.

Indicators of Relational Development

Thibaut and Kelley have suggested that preliminary exchanges take place which provide foresight into future exchanges. Their most recent work (Kelley and Thibaut, 1978) amplifies upon four later stages of development.

After initial exchanges, a person may decide to move further into the relationship. This first step is based upon feelings that the relationship will be rewarding, nonexploitative, and continuing. The exchange partner is thought to be dependent upon the exchange relationship, to have similar interests, and to act to provide mutual benefits.

At step 2, the person feels compelled to assure the *other* that rewards will be provided and that the other will not be exploited or abandoned. Such assurances often involve statements which indicate that one is also dependent upon the relationship, has the same interests as the other, and will act for their mutual benefit.

If all has gone well, there will be a commitment to the exchange relationship (step 3). The parties agree to expand the exchanges and may publicly commit themselves to the relationship. As a result of public commitment, other potential relational partners may back off and society becomes obligated to help maintain the relationship. For example, marriage is normally a public sign of an exclusive relationship and causes many potential relational partners to suspend active interest.

Finally, step 4 is the point at which the parties may continue with the exchanges with the certainty that future exchanges will be equitable and dependable.

While the four steps are useful ways of conceptualizing relational development, two theories have been developed which extend this approach. Levinger and his associates (Levinger and Snoek, 1972; Levinger, 1974, 1977, 1979; and Huesmann and Levinger, 1976) have argued that relationships exist at various levels of relatedness. At the zero level of relatedness, partners are completely unaware of the other's existence. However, environmental situations or needs for contact often cause people to approach one another. They may, for example, live in the same apartment building or have too few friends. As a result, a relationship moves to level 1 which is called awareness, but as yet no interaction occurs. The individual may admire the other from afar and evaluate the other's reward potential. If the admirer decides that the other person is likely to be an attractive exchange partner, the decision to interact may occur.

With interaction comes level 2 or what is called surface contact. Surface contact is similar to what Berger and Calabrese (1975) have referred to as initial interaction. The communication tends to be very ritualized and predictions about the other are based on stereotypes. The rules guiding the communication are likely to be imposed by cultural norms. The evaluation of the relationship is based upon how well each member enacts roles relative to other potential relational partners. If the interaction is not personally satisfying, the relationship may end. If, however, the parties find that they have important areas of commonality (needs, interests, attitudes), come to like each other based upon their interaction and/or are required to understand each other as persons rather than roles, then the relationship may move to level 3 or mutuality. At this level, two people are engaging in mutual self-disclosure. As a result, they come to know much about each other's personal histories as well as their role related behaviors. The communication rules tend to be developed by the individuals involved. The people become committed to attaining equity in profits. Because they have become increasingly committed to each other, costs of ending the relationship become increasingly higher. Thus, many factors affect relational development, including communication and exchange processes.

Recently, Levinger (1979) has extended his model into the area of relational dissolution. He suggests that relationships do not necessarily continue to escalate or grow. Indeed, most relationships decline rather than expand. He argues that relationships may end in the early formative stages or in the later stages of relational development. Relationships in the early stages of development may dissolve for a variety of reasons. Some never develop because structural barriers prevent the partners from communicating. People may move or become segregated from contact. Other relationships may end because relational partners find that their initial interactions do not result in expected rewards. Finally, relationships may never develop because of pressure from one's social network. Friends, parents, or any significant other may disapprove.

Relationships that have developed to the point of mutual commitment (e.g., marriage) may also dissolve. Levinger has suggested that declining attractions for one's relational partner, rising alternative attractions, and declining barriers to relational dissolution have contributed to the decline of some established relationships. Thus, any relationship at any point of development may enter into a declining stage in which commitments and communication decrease.

Altman and Taylor (1973) have developed a similar model called Social Penetration Theory. Just as in Levinger's model, relational development is thought to involve both changes in exchange and communication. They argue that a person's personality can be thought of as a series of concentric circles. The outer circles represent information about a person that is fairly visible and known to other people. It also represents traits that many people share (e.g., sex, age). As one moves deeper into the circles, the information becomes more unique and is less likely to be known to anyone other than the individual. Relational development is characterized by the mutual penetration of the personalities of relational partners. Quite simply, as two people come to know each other, they gain a greater volume of information and more intimate information.

Social penetration is a process which tends to move from superficial to intimate levels of exchange. As people acquire more knowledge about each other, they forecast the benefits of further knowledge acquisition. Thus, they are generally orienting toward moving to greater intimacy. However, after reaching a given level of intimacy, the partners also expand their knowledge of a variety of topics at that level. For example, a person may consider political views and religious beliefs to be at the same level of intimacy. When arriving at that level in the relationship, the couple may expand their discussions to include both politics and religion. It is also the case that relational partners may choose to continue their explorations of less intimate and previously discovered topics as well. Our day-to-day activities often require us to communicate about things that we have previously discussed and may even find boring.

Social penetration tends to occur on a gradual basis rather than all at once. It is hypothesized that the fastest rate of penetration occurs in the early and middle stages of relational development rather than in later stages. This may be due to the fact that later stages of development involve disclosure of high-risk intimate information which people rarely share with anyone.

The overall process of relational development is thought to be controlled by rewards and costs. The greater the ratio of rewards to costs and the greater the absolute magnitude of rewards, the greater the rate of penetration or relational development. This idea is central to Altman and Taylor's model. They suggest that the person is constantly assessing the rewards received from the relationship in the past, the current rewards being received and the likely rewards to be received in the future. A person attempts to keep track of relative gains and projected gains from the relationship. These assessments determine how fast or whether the relationship will continue to develop.

Finally, Altman and Taylor describe four stages of penetration. The first stage is called orientation and represents highly ritualized conversations where public information about self is disclosed. If the relationship is perceived to be rewarding, it then progresses to a second stage called exploratory affective exchange. At this stage, communication about public areas of personality is expanded and some movement into intermediate areas of personality occurs. However, discussion of these intermediate areas remains somewhat limited and proceeds cautiously. If the outlook for relational rewards remains good, the relationship moves to the third stage called affective exchange. At this stage, more information of a personal nature is exchanged and fewer areas of personal history are "off limits" for discussion. The last stage is called stable exchange, and is the point at which the relational partners know each other very well and, in most cases, can accurately predict each other's behaviors. Most topics, regardless of their intimacy, are available for discussion.

Thus, Kelley and Thibaut suggested that relational development consists of a series of steps in which the parties communicate assurances about the equitable and dependable nature of future exchanges. Levinger and associates and Altman and Taylor have expanded upon this notion by suggesting that increasingly intimate personal information is exchanged as the relationship develops. The exchange of increasingly intimate information may serve to assure the relational partner of one's sincerity and good faith in the exchange. One is trusting the other with personally private information and is also communicating information about how one views a variety of phenomena including exchange. As a result of knowing another very well, we should become more certain that our exchanges will be dependable and equitable.

Self-Disclosing Communication

Thibaut and Kelley do not explicitly deal with self-disclosure. However, their framework implies that self-disclosure plays an important role in social exchange.

They suggest that people are only partially constrained by their environment and abilities. People develop strategies for guiding their behavior so that they can achieve rewards given certain constraints. This strategy is reflected in the transformation they make of the given matrix into the effective matrix. The strategy in turn is based upon their dispositions (attitudes, intentions or values).

Self-disclosure would seem to imply the communication of two things: (1) the dispositions one has, and (2) the transformations (strategy) one is going to employ in this exchange. Since dispositions affect a person's strategy, we might assume that knowledge of dispositions might well allow us to predict the transformations.

However, such disclosures are risky. Self-disclosures might provide someone with information they might use against us. Certainly, disclosure that one generally tries to be cooperative may prompt relational partners to exploit our cooperative nature. In other words, knowledge that we try to maximize joint rewards consistently may prompt someone to avoid reciprocation, resulting in relational losses.

In addition, self-disclosure about our dispositions runs the risk that a person will describe to others how we normally guide our exchanges, resulting in relational losses in other exchanges. People then know how we transform the matrix, giving them an edge in exchanging with us.

Given these risks, we might expect that people will be cautious when disclosing information about themselves. Indeed, research on self-disclosure indicates that even a pervasive phenomenon such as the exchange of self-disclosure for self-disclosure only occurs under some conditions (see Altman, 1973; Taylor, 1979).

Thus, self-disclosure allows people to infer how another will behave in the social exchange. By releasing information about one's dispositions or strategies, one provides assurances of nonexploitation to one's exchange partner. Unilateral exchange runs the risk of leading to one's own exploitation.

FOA AND FOA'S RESOURCE THEORY

Foa and Foa focus on the resources exchanged between individuals. Consequently, their analysis of relational development is oriented toward how various resources contribute to changes in a relationship.

Interpersonal Attraction

While Foa and Foa do not provide a specific definition of interpersonal attraction, they do imply that it is a positive feeling for another (see Foa and Foa, 1974: 240). They suggest that this feeling is the result of considering a person to be a potential exchange partner. A person must be perceived as a willing supplier of resources and as having ample supplies of resources to exchange in order to be an attractive exchange partner. The notion that we have resources which another is likely to value is critical for exchange. While we may be very attracted to a person who possesses a great quantity of valued resources, we may find that the individual has little need for the resources we have to exchange. Consequently, an exchange relationship will not result.

The most important contribution made by Resource Theory is the notion that people are attracted to specific others based upon the resource the target person can provide. Consequently, a person whose current level of love is below the lower boundary of the person's optimal range may seek someone who has a great deal of love to give. Similarly, a person who has too little status may seek to associate with important others. Thus, we ought to be able to specify in advance what it is that attracts a person to another by looking at the needed resource and the ability of the target person to provide that resource.

In addition, Foa and Foa suggest that a person who possesses a great deal of one resource may also possess large quantities of similar resources. For example, a prestigious member of a group may be able to confer status upon another and may also have access to great quantities of information. A highly affectionate person may be able to provide valuable compliments (conferring status) as well as love. Therefore, a given individual may be attractive because of the ability to provide quantities of similar resources.

Indicators of Relational Development

Although Foa and Foa do not discuss relational development, their analysis suggests that relational changes should involve changes in resources being exchanged. Particularistic resources such as love, status, and services gain some of their value from the specific individual who provides them. Consequently, these resources are exchanged with a few people (usually in dyadic relationships) whom we know very well and trust. Indeed, one must know another very well in order to choose the form of love that is most valued by the recipient. Universalistic resources (goods, money, and information) are valued regardless of the giver. Consequently, they can be exchanged in a variety of settings.

Given that particularistic resources are exchanged primarily in close interpersonal relationships while universalistic resources are exchanged in all types of relationships, we might predict that the exchange of the former should increase as the relationship develops. In initial encounters, two people may be restricted to exchanges of goods, money, or information. Indeed, cocktail party chatter may simply impart superficial information between relational parties. If an acquaintance from a party become a friend, the exchange may move from providing information to status (compliments) and services (dates). Only after a steady exchange of universalistic and somewhat particularistic resources will two people trust one another enough to exchange the most particularistic resource: love.

Thus, knowledge of the variety of resources exchanged between two people should lead to an accurate assessment of the stage of the relationship. In beginning relationships, only a few resources (primarily universalistic ones) will be exchanged. In long-term relationships, a wider variety of resources (both universalistic and particularistic) will be exchanged.

Self-Disclosing Communication

Resource Theory can also be applied to the study of self-disclosure. Let us assume for the time being that self-disclosure is an example of love. Since Resource Theory predicts that resources are exchanged in kind, we would expect that self-disclosure would prompt self-disclosure from a recipient. As previously noted, research does indicate that people have a tendency to self-disclose when another self-discloses to them. However, Resource Theory also predicts that love comes in various forms. Consequently, when one self-discloses to another, the receiver could return love through some other means (e.g., through physical affection) and the exchange would still be satisfying. Therefore, self-disclosure may not always be exchanged in kind.

Further, Resource Theory predicts that if one cannot return a resource in kind, then a similar resource may be exchanged. A person who receives self-disclosing communications from another may respond with a similar resource such as status or services. Indeed, Berg and Archer (1980) have found that an appropriate and satisfying response to self-disclosure is sympathy. One might respond to a person's self-disclosure of negative information about self by stating, "You aren't that bad." In other words, people seek to increase the person's status. If the person self-discloses positive information, congratulations may result, thereby increasing status as well. Thus, the response to self-disclosure is more complex than generally thought.

Resource Theory also implies that self-disclosure might be related to relational development. As noted earlier, the exchange of particularistic resources is dependent upon having a great deal of personal information about another. Obviously, self-disclosure is an efficient way of obtaining that resource.

However, Resource Theory is limited in its ability to predict self-disclosing communication. Paramount among these limitations is the difficulty of determining what kind of a resource self-disclosure actually is. Foa and Foa treat self-disclosure of affection for another as love. However, we may disclose information about self that is unrelated to our affection for the receiver. For example, we may describe our feelings toward our parents to our spouse. While this act implies trust and affection for our spouse, it does not seem to be the same sort of love that is translated by directly telling someone we love them or showing love physically. Indeed, one might argue that some forms of self-disclosure are simply imparting information. They provide the receiver with information about how to act toward us.

While this problem may seem trivial to some, it does create prediction problems. As noted earlier, a strength of Resource Theory is that it predicts that self-disclosure may prompt a number of behavior responses other than itself. These responses might be similar resources. If self-disclosure is perceived as love, then status or services might be appropriately returned. However, if self-disclosure is categorized as information, then appropriate responses might be money or status. Thus, the prediction becomes ambiguous. It is necessary that researchers determine how self-disclosure is perceived by a given exchange partner in order to predict the likely response.

WALSTER, BERSCHEID, AND WALSTER'S EQUITY THEORY

Walster et al. argue that people try to maintain equity in their interpersonal relationships. They wish to keep their ratio of net gains (outcomes minus inputs) to inputs equal to the same ratio for a relational partner.

Interpersonal Attraction

Berscheid and Walster (1978) have defined interpersonal attraction as a person's tendency or proclivity to evaluate another person or symbol of another person in a positive way. Given the distress people feel in inequitable relationships, we might expect that they will be attracted to individuals with whom they expect equitable exchanges can and will take place. This tendency should result in matching between relational resources. People who are capable of providing a great deal of a resource may also seek people who can provide similar amounts, thereby maintaining equity.

Walster et al. (1978) indicate that people who are high in physical attractiveness or possess pleasing personalities are able to attract people who have the same traits. Their review of the literature suggests that matching occurs for the following traits: physical attractiveness, mental health, physical health, and intelligence or education.

However, equity can also be achieved through associating with a dissimilar partner. A person might be able to provide greater amounts of a dissimilar resource in order to compensate for the lack of a resource. Indeed, Walster et al. (1978) review literature which indicates that beauty may be exchanged for high amounts of dissimilar resources such as socioeconomic status, love and concern, and self-sacrifice. Thus, relationships occur between partners possessing dissimilar resources if they can provide sufficient quantities to make the exchange equitable.

Indicators of Relational Development

Walster et al. (1978) base their analysis of relational development on intimate relationships. Intimate relationships are defined by a number of characteristics. They typically involve intense liking or loving. Like Altman and Taylor (1973), Walster et al. assume that intimate relationships involve self-disclosure of a wide variety of personal characteristics as well as intimate characteristics. Because intimate relationships tend to involve long term commitments, equity may be hard to calculate. Equity is influenced by the previous history of resource exchange as well as the person's projected gains in the future. Unless we are intimately involved in the relationship, we may have difficulty acquiring this information.

Intimate relationships are also hypothesized to involve exchanges of a wider variety of resources than casual associations. The resources in intimate relationships can be exchanged for a variety of different resources, whereas exchanges in casual relationships are limited to the same resource type. But most importantly, the resources exchanged in intimate relationships tend to be of greater value to relational partners. Relational partners are better able and willing to provide valuable resources to an intimate partner than a casual one. Given the greater value of these resources, punishment administered between intimates should be more painful than that between strangers. In addition, the costs associated with terminating an intimate relationship tend to be higher.

Finally, intimate relationships are characterized by two people defining themselves as a unit. They understand each other very well and often react as a single entity rather than as two individuals.

As a relationship changes from casual to intimate, relational partners will feel greater positive affect for each other, share a greater variety of resources of greater value, and define themselves as a social unit rather than as two individuals.

However, Equity Theory does not go into much detail as to how the relationship develops. Based upon equity principles, Murstein (1971b, 1974, 1976, 1977) has created a theory of mate selection entitled Stimulus-Value-Role (SVR) Theory. SVR Theory suggests that people go through stages of relational development. At each stage, the relational partners are concerned with equity, but the focus of the equity changes.

Assuming that people have some choice as to their relational partners, the first stage of relational development is called the stimulus stage. At this point, the relational partners have little information about one another and may rely upon outwardly visible cues (e.g., physical attractiveness) to determine their desire for the relationship. People at the stimulus stages are seeking equity with their relational partner in these characteristics. As a result, Murstein has found that relational partners at this stage tend to perceive themselves and are perceived by outside observers as being similar in physical attractiveness. It is important to note that Murstein does suggest that some cues will be more important at this stage than others. Therefore, a person may seek equity with regard to a given cue despite dissimilarities in other areas.

Assuming that all has gone well at the stimulus stage, the relationship progresses into the value stage. At this point, relational partners begin exploring values that are likely to be relevant to the relationship. For example, the partners may become concerned with their mutual views on sex roles. Again, equity becomes an important consideration. People seek to expand their relationships with others who have values that are likely to be congruent with their own. Murstein cites research which indicates that people who successfully escalate their relationships into marriage tend to have a great deal of correspondence between their value systems concerning marriage.

If the value stage has indicated equity can be achieved, the relationship progresses to the role stage. At this point, the partners begin to evaluate the fit or compatability between their relational roles. Two people should become committed to their relationship to the extent that they adopt relational roles that allow for the maintenance of equity. If one person chooses to employ an exploitative role, then the other may choose to discontinue the relationship. Indeed, Murstein suggests that few relationships actually progress through all the stages.

Self-Disclosing Communication

We might expect that self-disclosure follows the same equity principle as other relational behaviors. Chaikin and Derlega (1976) have used Equity Theory to describe how self-disclosure operates in a relationship. A person who receives a self-disclosing communication but does not respond with self-disclosure creates inequity. The disclosing person has provided information inputs into the relationship with no resultant gains. The recipient has gained information from the exchange and sacrificed little. Therefore, the recipient's net gains are higher than those of the discloser. In order to avoid these inequities, reciprocity of disclosure should take place.

In support of the equity position, Chaikin and Derlega (1974) found that observers of self-disclosure exchange rated reciprocal self-disclosure as more appropriate than unreciprocated disclosures.

While this approach is interesting, equity may be difficult to determine. Recipients of disclosure may believe they have undergone significant cost simply by listening and considering other persons' disclosures. There are times when we feel that we cannot handle our own problems let alone the burdens of others. Therefore, we must consider a variety of receiver and source costs when predicting equity in self-disclosure.

At the outset of this chapter, we focused on communication phenomena in relational development. By and large, these communication perspectives focused on the information exchanges between people and how they decreased uncertainty about another. Acquiring more detailed information about each other corresponded to relational development.

Our analysis of the Social Exchange Theories indicated several conclusions about communication and relational development. First, exchanging information about each other may be related to relational development by either facilitating exchange of other resources or by simply being another area of exchange into which the relationship is expanding. Some of the theories suggest that understanding another may help us know what a relational partner finds rewarding and, more importantly, how a relational partner will likely reward us. Gaining information about another should make the exchanges more efficient. As they become more efficient, exchanges may expand into the other areas and the relationship will develop. On the other hand, communication may simply be another form of exchange. Since relational development is generally characterized as expansions of the areas of exchange, we may find that information exchange is just another expansion. It is guided by principles similar to the exchange of other resources.

Second, the descriptions of relational development vary among the Social Exchange Theories. Homans stresses relational development within the framework of operant conditioning. Interpersonal attraction and self-disclosure are behaviors that are repeated because they are reinforced. Blau suggests that relational development occurs as people choose partners from the relational marketplace. Attraction for another may be based upon the supply and demand for resources. As the exchange for those resources are successfully carried out, trust develops and the exchange relationship continues. Thibaut and Kelley suggest that attraction is based upon a sampling of outcomes and projected future benefits. To the extent that a person has valued resources and is willing to provide them, the relationship should be attractive. In order to determine the person's willingness, we often exchange personal information, thereby providing assurances for future exchanges. Foa and Foa suggest that relationships develop according to the needs people have for a resource and the available suppliers of that resource. Information about self might be conceptualized as a resource for exchange in and of itself and may be used to gain other resources. Finally, Walster et al. argue that relationships are formed according to their potential for equitable exchanges. We are attracted to people with whom we can engage in equitable exchanges. Our self-disclosures are also guided by equity considerations.

4

INTERPERSONAL CONFLICT

Chapter 3 focused on how relationships develop. Yet, we are aware that not all relational changes bring two people closer together. Often the inability to resolve conflicts within the relationship results in a decision to reduce commitment to the relationship and it declines rather than grows. Since deescalation of a valued relationship is often traumatic (Weiss, 1976), communication scholars have become interested in studying the methods people use to resolve their interpersonal conflicts. We discuss how the Social Exchange Theories treat interpersonal conflict and its resolution.

Blessed is he who expects nothing, for he shall never be disappointed.

Alexander Pope
1727

Although somewhat cryptic, the above quotation might seem like good advice at difficult times in our relationships. People *do* form expectations about their relationships and those expectations are *not* always fulfilled. Indeed, we might characterize these situations as interpersonal conflict. Because we have little choice but to form relationships in order to meet our self-interest, interpersonal conflict may be an inevitable part of our lives as we seek the best relationships. Instead of avoiding exchange relationships and their potential difficulties, we might be better advised to learn how to appropriately resolve conflicts.

Communication researchers have become increasingly interested in interpersonal conflict and its resolution. At least three books have been written which apply communication principles to conflict (Jandt, 1973; Miller and Simons, 1974; and Frost and Wilmot, 1978) and a number of articles have appeared which examine conflict processes (see Roloff, in press, for a review of this literature). In general, attention has been drawn to three conflict topics: the causes of conflict, methods of conflict resolution, and the effects of conflict resolution.

Frost and Wilmot (1978: 9) define interpersonal conflict as "an expressed struggle between at least two interdependent parties, who perceive incompatible goals, scarce rewards, and interference from the other party in achieving their goals. They are in a position of opposition in conjunction with cooperation." Their position is consistent with a variety of other conflict theorists outside of communication (e.g., Coser, 1956; Deutsch, 1973; Mack and Snyder, 1957; Filley, 1975). Conflict emerges when people find themselves behaving in ways that run contrary to each other's self-interest. They are unable to attain rewards.

Elsewhere (Roloff, 1976), I made a distinction between short-term and long-term rewards. Short-term rewards are objects or activities of seemingly little relational value. They often include everyday activities such as driving to work, sleeping in, dressing the baby, or reading the newspaper. In and of themselves, they seem like relatively minor occurrences during a person's normal routine. Their loss is often irritating but not likely to be catastrophic to the relationship. Long-term rewards are those objects or activities that are of primary importance to the continuation of the relationship. They may include relational values such as fidelity, companionship, emotional support, and love. A single incident (e.g., discovering an extramarital affair) which violates one of these values may prompt a relational crisis. Short- and long-term rewards may also be related to one another. The accumulation of short-term rewards may prompt the feeling that one has also attained some long-term reward. For example, the attainment of love might involve the frequency of sexual acts, number of verbal statements expressing love, or remembering key events in one's personal and relational history (e.g., birthdays and anniversaries).

The absence or denial of a reward is costly. One has lost something that was expected. The accumulation of such costs might also raise the value of short-term rewards. A person who consistently ignores a relational partner while working on an important project may suddenly find that merely mentioning the project is sufficient to create a significant manifestation of the conflict (i.e., an argument). This sudden eruption of wrath may be totally surprising to the recipient.

Sternberg and Beier (1977) studied the conflicts that emerged between husbands and wives after three months of marriage and after a year of marriage. They found that even in a relatively short span of time (nine months between pre- and posttest) the topics of conflict changed significantly. After three months of marriage, husbands reported, in order of importance, politics, religion, and money as the most significant conflict areas; nine months later they reported money as being the source of most conflict followed by politics and sex. Similarly, newlywed wives reported conflicts about friends, politics, and money after three months of marriage but nine months later reported the most significant conflict topic was money, followed by friends and sex. Indeed, this research suggested that sex, money, and concern for each other tended to be the most significant areas of disagreement for married couples. One might note that each of these areas represents a resource discussed by the Social Exchange Theories.

Communication researchers have also been interested in conflict resolution processes. Based upon the seminal work of Marwell and Schmitt (1967), many factors have been identified that influence the use of compliance-gaining techniques in interpersonal conflicts (Miller, et al., 1977; Roloff and Barnicott, 1978, 1979; Lustig and King, 1980; Sillars, 1980; Roloff, 1981). My own research has been concerned with influences on the intention to employ five modes of conflict resolution: physical aggression, verbal aggression, regression, revenge, and prosocial techniques (Roloff, 1978, 1980; Roloff and Greenberg, 1979a, b, 1980). Use of a conflict resolution technique is influenced by socialization, personality, and perceptions of the rewards and costs associated with each strategy. Situational cues have been found to influence the use of the techniques both in conjunction with and independently of an individual's personality.

Researchers have also been interested in the impact of these techniques on the interpersonal relationship. While we typically evaluate a conflict resolution technique based upon whether it helps us win an argument, we must also be concerned with the effect the strategy has on our relationship. Conflict resolution techniques might be categorized as pro- or anti-social depending upon their effect on the relationship (see Roloff, 1976, for complete discussion of this issue). Techniques which rely upon force or deception typically cause relational deescalation. Instead of openly discussing an issue, the source relies upon coercion or lies to gain compliance. The target person gains no greater understanding of the other person. Consequently, the relationship does not grow. Indeed, Tedeschi and Bonoma (1977) have argued that coercion is typically a "measure of last resort" because of the substantial costs of using such techniques. Couples who use conflict avoidance techniques (i.e., they create an impression of no conflict when there really is one) tend to have less understanding of each other and are less able to reach agreement than subject who openly discuss the conflict (Knudson, Sommers, and Golding, 1980).

Prosocial techniques involve the open discussion of issues. By communicating positions, the partners come to understand each other better. The relationship should escalate rather than decay.

It should be noted that this distinction does not imply that openness will always lead to a permanent relationship nor that force and deception always lead to divorce. Two people may come to understand each other so well that they realize they have irreconcilable differences. Their relationship has escalated in the information they share but their interactions may decrease. On the other hand, some marriages may continue for years with little understanding because of the couple's commitment to the institution, children, or parents and friends. The relationship never really escalates in the sense that the partners acquire little insight into each other.

Thus, conflict is not bad in and of itself. It allows relational partners to "clear the air." They have an opportunity to improve their relationship or, if all else fails, leave the relationship. However, not all modes of conflict resolution are good. In fact, the modes of conflict resolution are typically what give conflict a bad name.

Because of the importance of this area, the remainder of this chapter will focus on how the Social Exchange Theories analyze conflict. The discussion of each theory will be subdivided into three sections: (1) causes of interpersonal conflict, (2) methods of conflict resolution, and (3) effects of conflict resolution on the relationship.

HOMANS' OPERANT PSYCHOLOGY APPROACH

Just as in the case of relational development, the implications of Homans' perspective for the study of interpersonal conflict will stem from the principles of operant psychology. The processes embodied in his propositions should allow us to explain conflict behavior.

Causes of Interpersonal Conflict

Homans' (1961, 1974) propositions suggest two sources of interpersonal conflict. First, the "aggression-approval proposition" states that conflict is likely to arise when a person receives a punishment that was not expected or does not receive a reward that was expected. If those expectations are violated then we become angry and more likely to engage in aggression. The consequences of our aggressive behaviors become more valuable to us, making aggression more likely in the future.

A former student provided me with an excellent example of this form of conflict. He worked for a major shipping firm while going to school. This firm provides an efficient means for consumers and businesses to send important packages across wide geographical areas. As one can imagine, the company depends upon its employees to load trucks with packages as quickly as possible. Just before Christmas, business picks up dramatically as more people attempt to send gifts. This increase in volume prompts the loading managers to apply pressure on workers; but the loaders feel they are already working more efficiently and harassment by their supervisors is unexpected. They become angry and seek revenge. The loaders start packing trucks such that a space is left between the front of the bed of the truck and the first stack of boxes. When the driver puts the truck into gear, the first stack of packages falls into the space between the front wall and the entire load shifts forward, crushing everything in its way. As you can imagine, consumers who find their packages resembling accordions become angry, call the supervisors, and complain bitterly. Because the complaints come some time after the fact, the supervisors "take the heat" and have no one to specifically blame for the destruction. The loaders are pleased because they have "gotten even" and their aggression is reinforced.

In interpersonal relationships, many factors cause expectations to be violated. Often external events occur which make it difficult for our relational partners to provide us with the rewards we have come to expect for certain behaviors. For example, the birth of the first child often results in difficulties with resource exchange for the parents (LaRossa, 1971). The partners may discover that they no longer have the time or energy to provide resources such as sexual and emotional support. Unless the parents come to realize why previously reinforced behaviors are no longer producing the same outcomes, relational problems may result.

Another likely source of this form of conflict stems from Homans' "deprivation-satiation proposition." A resource may have been provided so often that it is no longer valued. Consequently, no rewards are forthcoming for usually reinforced behaviors.

The second form of conflict is suggested by Homans' analysis of distributive justice. Distributive justice assumes that people compare their profits with those of other people. People who have investments approximately equal to ours should have profits similar to our own. When the rule of distributive justice is violated in a direction opposite of our self-interest, we become angry. Presumably, we should act in some way to restore distributive justice.

Violations of distributive justice may occur as a result of several factors. Sometimes third parties provide rewards beyond the control of the individual. In work situations, the employer has the right to provide salaries based upon a variety of criteria. An individual may not accept these criteria as valid. Consequently, a person may receive greater rewards than we do even though we have equal investment and the person who receives the higher salary did not necessarily seek it.

Violations of distributive justice may also emerge because of the structure of our society. Even though husbands and wives may have equal investment in the marriage, the opportunities outside of marriage for men may result in greater profits for husbands than their wives (see Scanzoni, 1972).

Methods of Conflict Resolution

Homans does not provide a detailed description of how conflict may be resolved. Certainly, the "aggression-approval proposition" does suggest that violated expectations result in aggression, but we know that people can respond to conflicts in nonaggressive ways as well. Consequently, we shall focus on the implications of Homans' analysis for how people come to use certain conflict resolution techniques.

People learn to resolve conflict in a given way through two processes. As suggested by Homans' propositions, the use of a mode of conflict resolution should be highly correlated with its previous success. People who receive valued rewards as a result of their use of a mode of conflict resolution should use that mode in similar situations in the future. For example, the notion that aggressive behavior can be acquired through reinforcement is well established. Patterson, Ludwig, and Sonoda (1961) observed that children who were praised for hitting increased that behavior more than children not reinforced for hitting. Geen and Stonner (1971) report that men who were praised for administering potentially painful shocks to another became progressively more punitive than did men who were not reinforced for shocking behavior. Cowan and Walters (1963) discovered that boys who were intermittently rewarded for hitting a doll were more likely to continue hitting the doll even after reinforcement stopped than were boys who were consistently reinforced.

Stimulus generalization has also been observed with regard to the learning of aggressive behaviors. Walters and Brown (1963) discovered that boys reinforced intermittently for hitting a doll were significantly more likely to assault another boy than were boys who were consistently reinforced for hitting a doll, never reinforced for hitting, or underwent no conditioning at all. Several studies have found that individuals who are reinforced for verbal aggression are more likely to engage in physical aggression than individuals who are reinforced for stating positive or neutral comments about another (Lovaas, 1961; Loew, 1967; Parke, Ewall, and Slaby, 1972). In other words, reinforcement for one form of aggression is generalized to another.

Reinforcement for our conflict behaviors may come from several sources. Parents are likely to respond to our conflict behaviors with approval or disapporoval. Bandura and Walters (1959) observed that parents of nonaggressive boys provided no reinforcements for their sons' use of physical aggression, whereas the parents of violence-prone boys tended to discourage violence at home but encourage and reinforce aggressive behaviors of their sons toward others. Bandura (1960) found that the parents of inhibited boys tended not to reinforce any aggressive behavior on the part of their sons, but the parents of aggressive boys tended to tolerate aggression between the boys and their siblings and reinforced the use of aggression by the boys against other people outside of the family.

In addition to parents, conflict behaviors may also be reinforced by peers. Certain subgroups may provide reinforcements to individuals who are highly aggressive. Bandura (1973: 192) describes the violent tendencies of delinquent subcultures: "Among the personal qualities most highly prized in such groups are fighting prowess, toughness, ability to outsmart others, and a quest for excitement. Members are rewarded for fighting exploits and lose stature for faintheartedness in the face of insults and combat challenges." Thus, peer groups may bestow status upon individuals who engage in verbal and physical aggression.

Other than socialization influences, a major source of reinforcement for our conflict behaviors stems from the person with whom we are in conflict. To the extent that the other person's responses are rewarding to us, our conflict behaviors should be reinforced and subsequently repeated. Rausch et al. (1974: 201) discovered that married couples tended to generally reinforce each other's role-played conflict behaviors: "Most often we were struck by the almost exquisite intermeshing of individual husband and wife in creating an approach to a conflict between them. Generally, individuals who avoid, deny, or repress conflict are helped in this by their partners and, in turn, help their partners in these same modes. So, too, those who escalate conflict into punitive support by one partner will also generally be mirrored by the other."

Homans also has suggested that behavior can be learned through modeling as well as operant conditioning. In the latest edition of his book

(Homans, 1974: 24-25), he suggests that people can learn to imitate the behaviors of others. Indeed, Homans suggests that Bandura's Social Learning Theory (1971, 1973) might be a useful approach for predicting certain behaviors. Bandura and his associates have demonstrated that observed aggression will be imitated by children (see Bandura, 1973: 72-86 for an excellent review of this literature). In particular, witnessing a model engage in aggression that is rewarded or at least not punished tends to increase the likelihood of aggression by the observer (Bandura, 1965; Thelen and Soltz, 1969; Walters, Parke, and Cane, 1965; Rosekrans and Hartup, 1967). Research has even found that seeing a model's verbal aggression reinforced tends to increase the likelihood of the observer's physical aggression (Parke, Wiederholt, and Slaby, 1972).

Again, a variety of models for adoption of conflict behaviors are available. Steinmetz (1979) reviewed a large number of studies which relate forms of parental discipline to aggressive behaviors. In general, the research indicates that the use of physical punishment as discipline is highly correlated with a child's aggressiveness. However, parental discipline is not the only role model for conflict; some children may be raised in a family involving violence between their parents. Gelles and Straus (1979: 554) have noted, "If our estimates are correct, millions of children can directly observe and use as a role model physical violence between husbands and wives."

As noted earlier, individuals may learn conflict behaviors by observing their peers. If one is involved in a violent subculture, one will have the opportunity to observe violence.

Perhaps most controversial is the notion that an individual can learn conflict behaviors through observing television models. A variety of studies have focused on the relationship between media violence and aggression in viewers (see Comstock, 1975 for a review of this literature). In general, a moderate but statistically significant correlation exists between observing violent television role models and viewer's aggression. Recently, Roloff and Greenberg (1979a, b) found sizable correlations between the perceived use of a mode of conflict resolution (verbal aggression, physical aggression, revenge, regression, and prosocial techniques) by an adolescent's favorite television character and the adolescent's intention to use the same technique.

Roloff and Greenberg (1980) found that perceived use of physical aggression, verbal aggression, revenge, regression, and prosocial techniques by peers and parents were significantly correlated with adolescent intention to use the same technique. While adolescent viewing of a variety of television programs was sometimes significantly correlated with the use of the modes, the magnitude of the correlations were small and the relationships inconsistent.

Thus, individuals see a variety of conflict behaviors performed in their presence. Their own reinforcement history as well as observations of others increases the likelihood that the conflict mode will be employed. Indeed, Homans' theory would suggest that when certain stimuli are observed the appropriate conflict behavior should occur. Gelles (1972) found a variety of regularities occurred in the sequence of husband and wife violence. Violence tended to occur in the evening on a weekend, and most often took place in the kitchen. Violence was often preceded by alcohol consumption by the violent individual, and the victim often contributed to the scenario through behaviors such as nagging, verbal assaults, criticisms, and actual physical aggression. In other words, the cues that led to physical aggression were readily identifiable. Indeed, some victims became so adept at predicting the occurrence of violence based upon the presence of those cues that they would engage in preemptive violence to stop the scenario.

While Homans does not describe the methods of conflict resolution in great detail, his analysis of how these behaviors might be acquired is quite useful.

Effects of Conflict Resolution on the Relationship

Since Homans does not specify the alternative methods of conflict resolution, it is difficult to determine their individual effects. However, we might be able to infer the effects of nonreinforcing conflict behaviors on the relationship as a whole. In Chapter 3 we noted that Homans suggests that as a relationship develops, the areas of exchange expand. People who like each other based on successful exchanges tend to interact more and exchange moves into the area of attitudes. Homans also notes that when inconsistencies emerge in our exchanges, we might choose to interact less and reverse the previous history of rewarding exchanges. Therefore, we might argue that our inability to resolve interpersonal conflict in an appropriate manner may adversely effect other exchanges, thereby causing relational deescalation.

A number of scholars support the notion that unresolved conflict tends to escalate into the other areas. Filley (1975) has argued that the outcomes of a current conflict become part of the antecedent conditions for a later one. He classified outcomes into three types: win/lose, lose/lose, and win/win. Win/Lose outcomes are often produced by conflict resolution techniques such as force or deception. One person wins and another loses. The next conflict between the two is likely to be more intense as the loser attempts to redress losses. Lose/lose outcomes are produced by techniques in which individuals both sacrifice something. Compromise might produce such an outcome. Filley argues that such outcomes are not wholeheartedly accepted by the parties since both lost something. Therefore, future conflicts may involve attempts by both to redress their losses. Only win/win outcomes involve satisfactory antecedent conditions for future conflicts. Since both parties explored nonobvious solutions and refused to accept low quality decisions, we should expect them to be more satisfied with the resolution and value their relationship more.

Not only does the conflict resolution method influence later conflicts, it may also represent a source of conflict in and of itself. People often resent the way in which another seeks compliance. Brehm (1966) described a state called psychological reactance resulting from the attempts of another to limit one's freedom. Such a state is oriented toward restoring freedom by engaging in the threatened behavior or some equivalent behavior. Holmes and Miller (1976: 286) have noted: "Often the escalation of conflict occurs, not because of the degree or nature of the contrience between the individual's goals, but because of the way one or both of the participants pursue their goals. In other words, the means adopted to achieve an end often become as much of an issue as the end itself."

Finally, the method of conflict resolution might also influence other areas of exchange. Birchler, Weiss, and Vincent (1975) observed maladjusted and adjusted married couples in casual and experimental conditions. They found that distressed couples tended to engage in more negative reinforcing and fewer positive reinforcing communications than did nondistressed couples or strangers. In addition, distressed couples reported engaging in fewer activities with their spouse and more with other people than did nondistressed couples. In other words, it seems that they have limited their interaction. Perhaps this phenomena can be used to explain those of Sternberg and Beier (1977). They found that couples initially unhappy with each other after three months of marriage became increasingly unhappy over the next nine months. The difficulties of conflict may extend into other areas of the relationship. They found that initially disagreeing couples reported their important conflicts at three months were over money, children, and politics in that order. After one year of marriage, the conflicts shifted to friends, concern, and love and sex. The areas of conflict appeared to become more personal.

BLAU'S ECONOMIC APPROACH

Blau's analysis of interpersonal conflict stems from his notion of power and its relationship to norms of fair exchange. As in the case of relational development, the ability to supply resources that are in great demand is the key to understanding the dynamics of conflict.

Causes of Interpersonal Conflict

Blau (1964a) argues that conflict is inherent in exchange relationships. Because people are motivated to gain maximum rewards at minimum costs, they try to establish advantageous positions in a relationship. A person establishes a superior position in a relationship by having less commitment to the relationship than the relational partner. A person who has significant commitments or investments in a single relationship does not ordinarily develop alternative exchange relationships. With fewer alternative relationships, the person in the weaker relational position must conform to the demands of the superior person. If the weaker party does not acquiesce, then the powerful person can cut off the supply of resources, leaving the weaker person with nothing. In essence, we have just described what Blau defines as power. Blau (1964a: 117) defines power as the "ability of persons or groups to impose their will on others despite resistance through deterrence either in the form of withholding regularly supplied rewards or in the form of punishment, inasmuch as the former as well as the latter constitute, in effect, a negative sanction."

However, asymmetric power does not in and of itself constitute conflict. A social group develops norms for what constitutes a fair exchange. Only when a powerful person violates these norms is it likely that interpersonal conflict will occur. People feel that the more powerful person is misusing superior position to extract unfair returns from the weaker partner. If, however, the more powerful person exchanges resources in a way that is socially sanctioned, then no conflict will occur. The two people will see the exchange as justified, even though it may perpetuate the power differences. It should be noted, though, that power differences certainly increase the probability of conflict. Blau (1964a: 84) notes, "Whereas rewards experienced in the relationship may lead to its continuation for a while, the weak interests of the less committed or the frustrations of the more committed probably will sooner or later prompt one or the other to terminate it." Indeed, research by Hill, Rubin, and Peplau (1976) found that 54 percent of relationships in which one partner was more emotionally involved than the other tended to break up during a two-year period. In contrast, only 23 percent of the relationships involving mutual commitment broke up in the same time period. Both men and women were more likely to end a relationship when they were the less involved partner than when they were the more involved. While women were more likely than men to break up a relationship, these differences were particularly large when they were the more involved partner. Similarly, Peplau (1977) reports that people less involved in a relationship have more "say" in relational matters.

Scanzoni (1972, 1979a, b) has explored power differences in marriage using an analysis similar to Blau's. He argues that husbands tend to be more powerful than their wives. This power difference stems from the male's greater access to supplies of resources. Scanzoni writes (1972: 69), "It should come as no surprise that husbands are more powerful than wives in routine family decision-making as well as in conflict-resolution, and that higher-status husbands generally have the greatest amount of family authority. Power rests on resources. Husbands, because of their unique relationship to the opportunity structure, tend to have more resources (material, status), hence more power than wives. And the husbands who have most access to the sources of prestige and tangible rewards—those in the middle class—have more power than working-class husbands."

As noted by Blau, power differences between husbands and wives do not necessarily imply conflict. Indeed, Scanzoni (1970) has noted that in cases of a husband's high earning power, the wife tends to view his power as legitimate. Wives of lower-class men tend to view their husbands' attempts to exert power as illegitimate. In other words, the man with little income demands compliance, but the wife tends to view his demands as running contrary to standards of fairness prescribed by society. Husbands, in a traditional view, have the "provider role." The wife provides certain benefits to him because he provides economic support for her. When he does not, his demands for her resources violate standards of fairness, and conflict will likely occur. Scanzoni (1972) has suggested that low-income men are aware of their inability to provide rewards and because of their insecurity tend to become excessive and uncompromising in dealing with conflicts with their wives. They attempt to reassert their power through physical subjugation.

However, interpersonal conflict is not limited to people in lower income brackets. Anytime a person acts in an unfair manner, conflict should result. Scanzoni (1979a, b) has noted that women are changing in terms of their preferences for sex roles and these changes may create different perceptions of what constitutes fair exchange. Some women remain "gender-role-traditionals." They prefer continued role differentiation between husbands and wives. They feel comfortable with the husband in the provider role and themselves in a homemaker role. More women are moving toward "gender-role-modern" positions. These women prefer little differentiation and sex typing of behaviors. Scanzoni (1979a) reports data which explore this variable and wife's employment on the perception of interpersonal conflict.

Of interest here, Scanzoni found that nonemployed wives who were "gender-role-traditional" reported little conflict with their husbands when compared with nonemployed "gender-role-moderns." Scanzoni hypothesizes that "traditionals" accept "patriarchal ideology" and, consequently, are less likely to dispute their husbands. If they do argue with their husbands, they are more likely to give in. "Moderns" tend to be more likely to dispute their husbands given their nonacceptance of male prerogatives. They consistently challenge marital values and roles. In addition, nonemployed wives who have worked since marriage or are looking for outside employment are more likely to report conflicts with their husbands than their counterparts. While "gender-role-modernity" was not correlated with the report of conflict for employed wives, Scanzoni did find that the more income the husband earned, the more empathy the wife felt for his position and the less conflict wives reported. If the husband provided high income, then his demands would be considered more legitimate and conflicts less frequent.

Methods of Conflict Resolution

Since power imbalances increase the probability that an unfair exchange will take place, Blau's analysis of conflict resolution concerns the equalization of power. Before we discuss how power can be equalized, we must examine the method by which one person comes to dominate another in the first place. The primary mechanism for enhancing one's power over another stems from providing valuable, scarce resources. In other words, providing someone with resources that cannot be found elsewhere creates dependence. This dependence can be used as a lever to demand compliance in other areas. Blau (1964a: 118) writes, "By supplying services in demand to others, a person establishes power over them. If he regularly renders needed services they cannot readily obtain elsewhere, others become dependent on and obligated to him for these services, and unless they can furnish other benefits to him that produce interdependence by making him equally dependent on them, their unilateral dependence obligates them to comply with his requests lest he cease to continue to meet their needs."

Thus, accepting resources from another creates ambivalence. On one hand, it provides us with resources we need; on the other hand, it makes us subservient to another if we cannot repay that person. Indeed, some people may be prompted not to accept our repayment as a way of keeping us subservient. Given that people find it difficult to refuse a resource to begin with, power differences could be relatively easy to create.

However, a person in a weak power position relative to a relational partner is not entirely helpless. Since the basis of a person's power is the threatened denial of future rewards, Blau (1964a) suggests that a person has four options other than complying with the more powerful relational partner. First, the weaker person can provide the stronger with valued rewards in exchange for threatened ones. Instead of allowing the other to establish dominance by threatening to stop exchanges, the weaker person can offer resources of sufficient value so that the other will want to continue the exchange. However, this response assumes that the person with lesser power has sufficient quantities of strategic resources to exchange, and that the powerful person will accept the resources in exchange.

Second, the weaker person can attempt to gain resources elsewhere. Independence from a more powerful person can be established if one can obtain resources from other sources. The threat of cessation of resources is less viable if alternative supplies are available. However, this response is dependent upon the availability of alternative supplies. In other words, it is necessary that the more powerful person not have a monopoly on resources.

Third, the weaker person can attempt to coerce the other into giving resources. If the weaker person can use physical force against the more powerful person, then the other may give resources out of fear. Of course, this requires that the weaker person be able to use coercive tactics. Weaker individuals may band together to demand equity from more powerful persons.[1]

Finally, the weaker person can simply choose to do without the threatened resource. A relational partner may find that compliance is so costly that the person would be better off without the exchange relationship. However, this response assumes that the weaker person's desire for independence will lessen the need for the resource. The more powerful person may try to instill values that make the threatened resource so attractive that the person cannot do without it.

Scanzoni (1979a, b) has provided a slightly different analysis of how a person seeks to gain rewards in conflict. As noted earlier, he is primarily interested in how gender-role orientation influences power and conflicts in marriages. His research has identified seven bargaining strategies used by wives in conflict with their husbands. These strategies are presented in an order ranging from most individualistic (stresses wife's self-interest) to the most collectivistic (stresses the benefit to the total family). The most individualistic strategy was one in which the wife stressed that the husband should comply because it would be beneficial to her. A second individualistic strategy stressed the benefits to the husband if he would comply with the wife's request. A third somewhat individualistic strategy was one which stated that the wife would do something for her husband if he would comply now. A strategy that fell in the middle of the continuum was one which stated that the husband should comply because his wife has done so much for him in the past. In essence, he owes compliance to her. A fifth somewhat collectivistic strategy suggested that the husband should comply because it was only right and fair. The sixth and more collectivistic strategy suggested that it was the husband's responsibility or duty to comply. The final strategy was most collectivistic and stated that the husband's compliance would be in the best interest of the family.

Scanzoni's research indicates that "gender-role-modern" women tended to use individualistic strategies more than "gender-role-traditional" women. The "modern" was not willing to subsume the statement of her own self-interest into that of the entire family. "Traditionals" tended to bargain more collectivistically, assuming that if the family interest was served so was their own.

The data indicate that women who were "moderns," well educated, possessed many resources, and were married to men who were also "moderns" tended to have "balanced" marriages. They were less likely to press persistently their claims against their husbands, to feel resentment against their husbands, and to be physically aggressive toward their husbands than "traditionals." However, not all "modern" wives are successful and happy bargainers. Those "moderns" who are married to traditional husbands tend to experience the same frustrations of traditional wives.

Thus, the methods of conflict resolution may also be influenced by how one views what is fair. If one rejects the validity of the basis for power differences, then one will likely press for one's own interests, whereas those who accept them may attempt to seek compliance within the power structure.

Unlike Homans, Blau provides little analysis of how a given method of conflict resolution is chosen. Given his orientation toward economics, we

might expect that people will tend to use the method that they expect will
create the greatest outcomes with the least costs. A similar analysis has
been suggested by Tedeschi and his associates (Tedeschi, Bonoma, and
Schlenker, 1972; Tedeschi, Schlenker, and Bonoma, 1973). They argue
that people seek compliance from others by the use of four sets of
techniques. First, people often threaten to deny future resources or
promise to give resources contingent upon whether another complies.
Second, people seek compliance by suggesting that the target will suffer
losses from external sources for not complying (warning) or will gain
rewards from others for complying (mandations). A third set of strategies
involves information control, where a person attempts to control the
amount and accuracy of information another has. The final set of strategies involves reinforcement control, where the person structures the
rewards and cues in a situation so that another behaves in ways which have
been previously reinforced.

The source of influence chooses the strategy that is most likely to gain
positive outcomes and avoid costs. Recently, Sillars (1980) demonstrated
that compliance-gaining techniques are chosen based on estimates of their
promise for relational rewards and costs. Similarly, the receiver of open
strategies such as promises, threats, mandations, and warnings decides
whether to comply based upon the magnitude of the punishment or
reward involved and the likelihood that it will be produced. In this model,
both sources and receivers behave in a manner which maximizes their own
rewards.

Effect of Conflict Resolution on the Relationship

Blau provides little discussion of this topic. Presumably, methods that
perpetuate inequities lead to the destruction of the exchange relationship.
Scanzoni (1979a, b) believes that as people become more "modern" in
terms of gender-roles, the likelihood of equitable relationships increases,
resulting in greater solidarity of interpersonal relationships. Given this
position, we might expect that methods which prompt mutually satisfying
or profitable outcomes will lead to relationship expansion.

THIBAUT AND KELLEY'S THEORY OF INTERDEPENDENCE

While Thibaut and Kelley provide some discussion of conflict in their
initial work (Thibaut and Kelley, 1959), Kelley's recent work (Kelley,
1979, and Braiker and Kelley, 1979) provide refinement of their position.

In essence, conflict involves response interference and different interpretations of why the interference took place.

Causes of Interpersonal Conflict

It is important to remember that Thibaut and Kelley (1959) argue that people in interpersonal relationships are interdependent. The behaviors that they perform toward each other influence their mutual outcomes. Consequently, the possibility exists that people may engage in incompatible behavioral sequences. In other words, one or both parties engage in behaviors that increase their costs or make the attainment of rewards less likely.

As noted earlier, relational partners who are similar in values and roles have a greater likelihood of marrying each other. However, similarity is not likely to be found in all traits. For example, a wife might enjoy going to the opera, and particularly enjoy going to the opera with her husband. Assume that the couple go to the opera and the husband falls asleep and begins snoring. According to Thibaut and Kelley, the husband's behavior is likely to be costly to his wife, and therefore, incompatible with the wife's behaviors. It interferes with her reward attainment for several reasons. Since enjoying the opera involves focused attention, his snoring may distract her and draw attention from others, creating social embarrassment. Finally, she enjoys going to the opera because she hopes he will enjoy it as well. His lack of attention may create disappointment, guilt, and embarrassment.

While this example represents interference on the part of the husband, conflict over the rewards in a given situation may result from mutual interference. The husband may have preferred to have stayed at home and her insistance that they go to the opera interfered with his reward attainment.

If the conflict remained at the level of the given matrix it might be easily resolved. A simple nudge might awaken the husband. However, Kelley (1979) argues that conflicts often escalate into areas defined by the dispositional matrix. In other words, the wife may interpret his sleeping as being caused by a variety of dispositions. For example, she may conclude that he is crude and boorish. She might perceive that his sleeping is inconsiderate of her needs, and consequently interpret his behavior as a lack of love. Finally, she might define his behavior as vindictiveness. Since he really did not want to go to the opera anyway, he is attempting to "get even" with her.

This type of conflict is called attributional conflict. People attempt to determine why others perform in certain ways. Their typical conclusion tends to be that their relational partners behave the way they do because of some stable disposition or trait. This is particularly true when the other person has engaged in negative behavior (see Cunningham, Stambul, and Kelley, 1973; Tiggle, Peters, and Kelley, 1977; both cited in Kelley, 1979: 18-23). Conflict emerges when we compare the attributions made by the observer of negative behavior and the source. Orvis, Kelley, and Butler (1976) asked couples to report instances of their behaviors in which they developed different reasons for the behaviors. The data indicated that the majority of these instances involved negative behaviors by one of the partners. When examining the explanations for the negative behaviors, attributional conflict was apparent. The person who received the negative behavior tended to explain the behavior by attributing it to the source's personal characteristics, attitudes, or ulterior motives. The source of the behavior tended to explain the event by either finding excuses for the behavior (e.g., extenuating circumstance, other people, or physical/psychological states caused the behavior) or presenting reasons which justified the behavior (e.g., the behavior was really in the receiver's self-interest or the source thought the behavior was for the best). In other words, the recipient of the negative behavior tends to blame the source for the consequences, whereas the source blames the situation or the receiver for inaccurately perceiving the situation.

In addition, attributional conflict may occur because of the tendency of people to assume that they take into consideration their partner's needs more than the partner considers theirs (Ross and Sicoly, 1978). In other words, the transformations made by the two relational parties tend to be misunderstood; each believes that the other is relatively insensitive and more self-interested.

Thus, two relational partners are likely to disagree when their behaviors are incompatible or when they perceive that the incompatible behaviors are produced by different causes. Consequently, conflict likely begins with the discussion of a specific event and then escalates into conflict over broader causes. In this process, the two parties may cite other factors that also reflect their perceptions of the cause of the conflict. The wife, for example, may point out that her sleeping husband has also been arriving home late at night and has been generally unresponsive to her in conversation. The husband may indicate that his work load has increased lately causing him to be exhausted in the evenings. His unresponsiveness is due to external causes, not internal disposition.

Methods of Conflict Resolution

Since conflict is costly and drive-producing, Thibaut and Kelley (1959) argue that people try to avoid it. They may develop ways of synchronizing their behaviors so that interference is removed. The wife may plan to go to the opera on weekends when the husband is not as tired and the husband may promise to avoid working on the weekend so he will not be tired. They may also find ways of eliminating the interfering behavior. The husband may take some stimulant (e.g., a quart of coffee) before going to the opera. In other words, the husband and wife may figure out how to transform their outcomes into patterns that reduce interference.

However, determining the appropriate transformations to make is not an easy task. The easiest way would be to have couples openly communicate with one another about the changes that ought to be made. Indeed, experimental evidence presented by Steinfatt and Miller (1974) indicates that people in an experimental game involving highly discrepant outcomes learn to redistribute the outcomes in a mutually beneficial manner if they are allowed to communicate. But communication is not an absolute guarantee that the problem will be solved. Recently, Tedeschi and Rosenfeld (1980) noted that bargainers may be tempted to disguise their goals in interaction. Relational partners already in conflict may not openly describe what they want for fear of exploitation. As a result, inexact communication makes for further conflict.

Consequently, we might expect that conflict is never entirely resolved. The most people can hope for is to roughly estimate the other's needs and then adapt their behaviors accordingly. If the behavior is appropriate, then the interaction may proceed almost automatically with little need for explicit discussion. Relational rules will guide the exchange.

While the description of interpersonal conflict implies that conflict is threatening to a relationship, Braiker and Kelley (1979) have argued that conflict may be part of relational growth. While not all couples report disagreement during relational development, conflict may facilitate relational growth in a number of ways. Relational conflict may prompt the partners to change their association in an innovative and rewarding manner. They find new and better paths to need fulfillment. Conflict may also increase the parties' commitment to the relationship. After resolving a conflict, the parties may feel even closer. The adage that "the best part of breaking up is making up" may be true. In addition, relational parties attempting to resolve a current conflict may also develop rules that aid in the resolution of future conflicts. Finally, interpersonal conflict may contribute to feelings that the relationship is unique. The individuals have solved problems together in ways that may be different from other people. Successful conflict resolution may even be remembered in a nostalgic light.

Thus, conflict may be destructive to some relationships but not to all. Indeed, conflict may even be a sign of stability. Coser (1956: 85) has similarly noted, "Stable relationships may be characterized by conflicting behavior. Closeness gives rise to frequent occasions for conflict, but if the participants feel their relationships are tenuous, they will avoid conflict fearing it might endanger the continuance of the relationship." Thus, lack of conflict does not always indicate relational stability.

The Effect of Conflict Resolution on the Relationship

The only discussion of the effect of a mode of conflict resolution on the exchange relationship is provided by Kelley (1979). He suggests that the way a person resolves a conflict can become an issue of conflict itself. In particular, several studies have found that male and female relational partners differ in the way they resolve conflicts with each other (Crawford et al., 1977; Kelley et al., 1978). Males tend to be conflict avoiders. They attempt to make the conflict logical and devoid of emotion, but at the same time tend to get angry. Women tend to become frustrated as a result of the male's delay tactics and emotionally press the conflict further. Since women become more upset about emotional factors in the relationship, the attempts of men to remove emotion from the conflict exacerbates the conflict. Since men tend to be focused on external tasks, they often attempt to avoid being distracted by other concerns. When the female attempts to continue to press the issue, the husband is forced to deal with it and the conflict is expanded further.

Consequently, the modes of conflict resolution may themselves be a form of response interference that escalates the conflict.

FOA AND FOA'S RESOURCE THEORY

Foa and Foa (1974) more than the other theorists introduce communication into the conflict process. Misperception in communication represents an important source of conflict in a relationship.

Causes of Interpersonal Conflict

Resource Theory identifies two major sources of conflict. First, conflict occurs when a person denies another a resource, creating some need. As noted earlier, Foa and Foa believe that people have an optimal range for each of the resource categories. When their current possession of a resource drops below the lower bound of the optimal range, they feel a need and seek more of that resource. When a person who has been a dependable source of rewards cuts off the supply, we can expect inter-personal conflict to occur as the need for the resource becomes acute. The deprived person becomes increasingly frustrated.

Second, conflict may be a result of distortion in interpersonal commu-nication. Interpersonal communication is often the medium for trans-mitting resources. Love can be easily transmitted verbally and through a variety of nonverbal cues (Argyle, 1975). Status can be transmitted through compliments. Information is inherently provided via communica-tion.

In addition, interpersonal communication may be a mechanism for describing to another the meaning of some resource we give. We often enclose cards expressing how our gifts to relational partners reflect our love for them.

Conflict emerges when two people are unable to understand the resources being transferred. Two forms of misunderstanding are identified. First, the source and receiver may use different "mapping rules" to determine what a resource is. In other words, two people may have different interpretations of what resource is being transmitted via commu-nication. For instance, this author heard a man communicating with his future daughter-in-law. He indicated that she was now joining his family and should anything happen to his son, she could depend upon him for emotional and financial support. From his perspective, he was sending love to her. However, she perceived the statement from a different perspective. Rather than extending love, the statement implied that she was unable to provide for herself. She could not survive alone so she was marrying someone to care for her. In essence, the statement was interpreted as a denial of status rather than an expression of love. However, the woman realized her future father-in-law's intent and no conflict emerged.

A second misunderstanding is called "mismatching." This problem emerges from the ability of a source and receiver to differentiate between resources. Some people are able to see the six types of resources as being separate and distinct categories, while others may not see much difference between the categories. A person may see love and status as being two separate resources. Consequently, that person may continue to feel affec-tion for another even though the other person is not talented in some area (e.g., one lacks status as a cook, repairperson, and so forth). Another who sees compliments as being the same as expressions of love may come to be in conflict with a person who sees the two as being quite separate. Therefore, people have a tendency to compliment their loved ones for talents they may not really have as a way of avoiding conflict.

Methods of Conflict Resolution

The major method of dealing with conflict arising from the denial of a resource is through retaliation, by denying that person the same or similar resources. If a dissimilar resource is denied, then the intensity of the denial is increased and subsequent residual hostility is increased (Donnenwerth and Foa, 1974).

Foa and Foa (1974) have identified three ways in which a person may retaliate to reduce the level of frustration resulting from being denied a resource. The first method is called direct retaliation. In this form of retailiation, the person denied a resource retaliates against the same person who previously denied the resource. The second method is called displacement. Displacement involves retaliating against some third party rather than the individual who denied the resource. The final method is called vicarious retaliation. With this form of retaliation, the person who denied the resource is retaliated against by a third party rather than the victim. In essence, the victim finds an authority figure or loved one to retaliate against the exploiter. Foa and Foa argue that the three forms of retaliation are differentially effective at reducing the victim's frustration. Direct retaliation appears to be the most satisfying form of revenge. Displaced retaliation appears to be ineffective at reducing frustration, and vicarious retaliation actually appears to increase frustration.

When conflict is due to interpersonal communication difficulties, some kind of explanation of resource categorization must occur. This may involve greater amounts of time and energy explaining one's statements than would normally occur. Both source and receiver need to be concerned with each other's intentions in the communication situation, otherwise inadvertent conflict may arise.

Effects of Conflict Resolution on the Relationship

While Foa and Foa do not specifically discuss how retaliation affects the relationship, we might infer that the resource used to retaliate may indeed deescalate the relationship significantly. People who have close interpersonal relationships and discover that one or both have been sexually active with other people may seek to retaliate by denying the other the same or similar resources. If infidelity is defined as a denial of love, then the victim may choose to deny expressions of love to the exploiter or establish frequent sexual contacts with others. If unable to retaliate this way, the victim may choose to deny the exploiter services (e.g., refuse to take care of the other) or status (e.g., spread the word that the partner is a philanderer). In any case, the form of retaliation may indeed deescalate the relationship further. We might expect that retaliation may lead to further retaliation in the same or similar resource areas by the exploiter and the relationship continues to decay.

Gottman et al. (1976) found that unresolved conflicts lead to misunderstandings of communication between relational partners. While couples whose marriages were characterized as distressed were just as likely as nondistressed couples to send each other messages intended to be viewed as positive, the distressed couples interpreted each other's communications as being more negative than did nondistressed couples. Thus, couples already in conflict with each other are more likely to interpret (i.e., use different "mapping rules") their communications as negative even when they are intended to be positive. This process leads to more conflict and the relationship decays.

WALSTER, BERSCHEID, AND WALSTER'S EQUITY THEORY

Walster, Berscheid, and Walster (1976) focus on conflict arising from inequity and the attempts to restore equity. They probably provide the most detailed description of conflict and its resolution.

Causes of Interpersonal Conflict

Equity Theory assumes that interpersonal conflict arises in a relationship whenever people perceive inequities in the distribution of profit. Propositions 3 and 4 of the theory suggest that when people find themselves in an inequitable relationship, they become distressed, and the greater the inequity, the greater the distress and subsequent attempts to restore equity. In addition, they assume that the victim of an inequity tends to feel more distress than the harm-doer (person who benefits from the inequity). Further, inequities that are intentionally produced by a relational partner create more distress and prompt stronger attempts at equity restoration than do inequities that are accidentally or unintentionally created.

Chapter 3 indicated that researchers have found that people tend to be attracted to others with whom they can have an equitable relationship. Consequently, we might assume that a relationship should be relatively conflict-free, since equity was a primary consideration in its formation. However, inequities often occur regardless of our attempts to form relationships that will be equitable.

Walster, Walster, and Berscheid (1978) suggest three reasons why inequities may occur in a previously equitable relationship. First, as a relationship develops, people come to learn more about one another. Since it is doubtful that even at the time of marriage or cohabitation a person knows everything about another, the learning process continues even after the relationship is institutionalized. Therefore, we may discover new information about relational partners that create inequities we had not planned for. Altman and Taylor (1973: 168) have similarly noted, "Two people come to know, and deal with one another in very personal areas; they are also very dependent on one another for physical, social, and emotional support and have become important to one another. On a sheer probability basis, therefore, more extensive interaction should result in greater opportunities for conflict and disagreement." This greater probability for conflict may be reflected in the finding of Birchler, Weiss, and Vincent (1976) that both distressed and nondistressed married couples transmitted more negative and less positive messages to each other than strangers. Married couples may know each other so well that they have more to disagree about.

Second, people often change during a relationship. Needs do not stay the same. Given the propensity of couples in close relationships to rely upon restricted syntactical codes (see Chapter 1), these changes may not always be communicated to the relational partners. We may assume that our relational partners understand the changes we go through when they really do not. Consequently, an inequity may occur quite to the surprise of both relational partners.

Third, inequities may occur as a result of dramatic changes in the relationship resulting from important events. As noted earlier, the birth of a baby may result in an inequitable relationship until the parents are able to adjust.

While not discussed by Walster, Walster and Berscheid (1978), I would add a fourth cause of inequity. We may suddenly come to believe that the distribution of profits which we once viewed as equitable are no longer equitable. In other words, the ratio of outcomes may not change, but we evaluate them differently. Several factors may cause us to change our evaluation of the current distribution of outcomes. First, external change agents (friends or parents) may convince us that our current outcomes are actually unfair. Scanzoni (1972: 85) writes, "A major thrust of Neofeminism, or Women's Liberation, is precisely that—to create feelings of relative deprivation among traditional women. Women in the movement obviously want other women to feel deprived vis-à-vis men, but they also want them to feel deprived compared to women who are fulfilling more modern behaviors."

I have suggested elsewhere (Roloff, in press) that the mass media may have an impact upon relationships by defining certain current exchange patterns as being inequitable. The media may convince people that their current relationship is inequitable and that others feel that is inequitable also. Thus, dissatisfaction with distribution of outcomes may arise due to changes in the way we view the outcomes we have, rather than actual changes in the quality of outcomes.

Methods of Conflict Resolution

In discussing conflict resolution, Walster, Walster and Berscheid (1978) focus upon the reactions of the harm-doer, the victim, and outside observers to inequity. Equity Theory assumes that the harm-doer tends to feel distressed by an inequitable relationship while the beneficiary of the inequity. The harm-doer may fear that the exchange relationship will be threatened because the victim may wish to leave it, or may fear retaliation by the victim or outside interested observers. Consequently, the harm-doer should also be prompted to find a way to restore equity.

The harm-doer may use two general mechanisms to restore equity. The most obvious mechanism for restoring equity is to attempt to actually bring the ratio of profits back into balance. The exploiter may provide the victim with compensation so that the victim has more rewards and fewer costs *or* the exploiter may voluntarily decrease personal rewards and increase personal costs so that net gains are similar to those of the victim's. Thus, a husband who feels that his wife is bearing too much of the load of housework may hire a maid to help her (increase her rewards and lower costs) or take over a greater share of the household duties himself (increase his own costs).

However, the harm-doer may also choose to restore psychological equity rather than actual equity. The harm-doer may blame the victim for the inequity, minimize the suffering of the victim, deny personal responsibility for the inequity, or apologize to the victim. The husband may justify the inequity by stating that his wife is the one who freely chooses to engage in more of the housework and actually enjoys it.

Two corollaries to their propositions explain which method of equity restoration the harm-doer will choose. Corollary 2 of proposition 1 states, "Other things being equal, the less costly an exploiter perceives an available equity-restoring device to be, the more likely he is to use this technique to restore equity." Corollary 1 of proposition 4 states, "Other things being equal the more adequate an exploiter perceives an available technique to be, the more likely he is to use that technique to restore equity" (Walster, Walster and Berscheid, 1978: 36).

Thus, a harm-doer will seek to restore equity in a manner that also serves self-interest. Therefore, Equity Theory predicts that harm-doers will tend to use compensation or justification techniques to restore equity. However, harm-doers will tend to avoid justification techniques if they involve too great a distortion of reality or if the harm-doers anticipates a great deal of interaction with the victim or the victim's cohorts in the future. In those cases, we might expect restoration of actual equity through compensation to take place.

As noted earlier, the victims of an inequitable relationship tend to be more distressed by the inequity than the harm-doer. Their responses to the conflict may be to demand compensation from the harm-doer, retaliate against the harm-doer, or find justifications for the inequity. The last method of equity restoration seems strange. Why would the victim come to accept the inequity? Possible reasons may be that the victim perceives no better alternatives, or the victim may find that accepting self-blame for the inequity may provide a feeling of control over future occurrence. The victim can say, "I caused the inequity myself and will never allow it to occur again." Regardless of the reason, we sometimes observe the victim accepting personal responsibility for the inequity. Gelles (1972) found that battered wives often engaged in self-blame for their beatings.

Sometimes external agents may choose to become involved in an interpersonal conflict. Women's groups are attempting to provide private and public support for women in distress. Certainly, parents may become involved in the conflicts between their children or between their adult children and spouses. The outside agents have several methods of attempting to restore equity. They may prod or force the harm-doer to make restitution to the victim. Outside agents may punish the harm-doer or provide compensation to the victim. In essence, the external agents form coalitions with the victim. However, the external agent may also form a coalition with the harm-doer. Scanzoni (1972) has argued that regardless of the issue, marriage counselors have a tendency to agree with the husband rather than the wife. The assumption of many therapies is that the wife should adapt to the husband (see Figes, 1970, for a more detailed analysis of this bias). Thus, an external agent may not always be a source for restituion but for justification of the inequity.

Effect of Conflict Resolution on the Relationship

Walster, Berscheid and Walster, (1976) do not discuss the impact of individual equity-restoring devices upon the relationship. They do suggest, however, that success in restoring equity is important to maintaining the relationship. Research by Berscheid et al. (1973) demonstrated that people in more equitable relationships tended to be happier, more content, and less angry than those in inequitable relationships.

However, this position should be somewhat modified. Burgess and Nielsen (1977) have reviewed a number of experimental studies in which inequity resulted in a *stable* exchange relationship when the victim found the inequitable relationship to be more profitable than alternative relationships. In addition, an equitable relationship was stable only if the outcomes of the relationship were better than alternative relationships. Therefore, restoration of equity may be a necessary but not sufficient condition for the continuation of the relationship.

At the beginning of this chapter, we noted that communication scholars have been interested in causes of conflict, the methods used to resolve conflict, and the effects of those methods on the relationship. The Social Exchange Theories concur that conflict emerges when an expected reward is not provided or when one perceives oneself as receiving less profit from the relationship than a relational partner of equal investment. These two instigators of conflict may occur because of changes in the actual distribution of resources or changed perspectives of whether the established distribution pattern is indeed fair.

As a result, the Social Exchange Theories suggest that methods are employed to resolve the conflict. These techniques may involve attempts to restore one's power, communication about one's needs, or the establishment of actual or psychological equity. The use of these methods may be a consequence of one's previous history of rewards and punishments or one's expectation that the technique will be rewarding.

Finally, if the strategy effectively restores the exchange of resources or restores equity to the resource exchange, then the relationship will continue. If resources are not forthcoming and the partners have viable relational alternatives, the relationship may decay.

NOTE

1. One might argue that our legal system is a tool for forcing powerful people to be fair in their dealings. However, our legal system might also be used to protect powerful people from the force of weaker ones banded together.

5

A CRITICAL ASSESSMENT

In the preceding chapters, we have examined how five Social Exchange Theories view interpersonal communication. Now, it is necessary to evaluate the utility of these approaches by focusing on the strengths and weaknesses of the perspectives.

I pass with relief from the tossing sea of Cause and Theory to the firm ground of Result and Fact.

Sir Winston Churchill
1898

The sentiment expressed in the above quotation may seem to contradict the one which opened Chapter 2. There, Lewin noted that there was "nothing so practical as a good theory." The apparent contradiction may be resolved by noting that Lewin emphasizes the word "good." Not all theories provide accurate explanations or predictions of human behavior. In order to determine how "good" the Social Exchange Theories are, we will present their strengths and weaknesses. Since there are many commonalities, we examine them as one theoretical approach, noting special cases along the way.

STRENGTHS

Six strengths emerge from the discussion of the perspectives.

First, the perspectives are constructed in a more formalized manner than many theories used in communication. As noted, scholars differ on what a theory is. However, they do agree that the more formalized the theory, the better. With two exceptions (Blau's Economic Approach and Thibaut and Kelley's Theory of Interdependence), the Social Exchange Theories consist of propositions relating key variables to one another. Homans (1961, 1974) advances a set of propositions arising from operant psychology. Foa and Foa (1976) suggest two propositions which describe resource exchange. Walster, Berscheid, and Walster (1976) have formulated five propositions which focus on equity and its restoration. While Blau (1964a) and Thibaut and Kelley (1959) do not advance specific propositions, their analysis parsimoniously describes social exchange.

Second, while our analysis has not attempted to logically deduce hypotheses from the propositions, we have been able to infer a variety of implications for interpersonal communication phenomena from the perspectives. They have either directly addressed the phenomena or have been suggestive of how we might extend the theory into other areas.

Third, the perspectives are applicable to interpersonal communication in a variety of contexts. Indeed, several research projects have examined social exchange in organizational settings (see Walster, Walster, and Berscheid, 1978: 114-142 for a review of these studies) and a number of theorists have focused on exchange as a basic process in marriage (Nye, 1978, 1979; Scanzoni, 1979a, b).

Fourth, the perspectives all have included suggestions of how their hypotheses may be studied. Often theories ignore issues concerning methodologies that might be used to test them. Homans (1961, 1974) focuses on the empirical methods associated with experimentation in operant psychology. Blau (1964a) implies that econometric methods are useful. Thibaut and Kelley (1959) tie their theory closely to methods used in the study of experimental games. Foa and Foa (1974, 1976) employed traditional experimental designs in their research on resource exchange. Finally, Walster, Walster, and Berscheid (1978: 232-245) have described the questionnaires they have used to explore equity and reactions to inequity.

Fifth, the Social Exchange Theories suggest a variety of policy implications that may be used to alter our environments. Blau (1964a), for example, has provided detailed descriptions of the effect of power on a relationship and how a weak person may attempt to be independent of more powerful partners. Scanzoni (1979a, b) has made a number of recommendations about the future of marriage and the roles of husbands and wives based upon Social Exchange Theory. In addition, a number of therapists have found social exchange principles useful ways to characterize marital difficulties and suggest positive changes (e.g., Patterson and

Reid, 1970; Strayhorn, 1978). The Social Exchange Theories are not simply academic tools, but could have some bearing on the improvement of everyday lives.

Finally, it seems that the Social Exchange Theories are based upon principles that people find consistent with their everyday experiences. We often find people describing their interactions in terms of enjoyment or displeasure. Individuals sometimes describe why they choose a behavior based upon how the behavior will help them achieve some reward. As noted earlier, research on the causes of interpersonal conflict often finds people reporting that the way resources are distributed is an important instigator of conflict. In my own teaching, students find the principles of social exchange easily applicable to their interactions.

Thus, the approaches provide benefits for both communication researchers and practitioners.

WEAKNESSES

Before we move into the specific weaknesses, several things should be noted. First, the list of weaknesses will be longer than the list of the strengths described earlier. This should not be a basis for prejudging or discounting the theories negatively. Some of the weaknesses are not as severe as the number of pages used to describe them might suggest. Second, the list of weaknesses consists of indictments drawn from literature concerning the Social Exchange Theories as well as those I have heard colleagues and students voice. In some cases, I have included arguments that may seem relatively weak but have been frequently mentioned. Indeed, some may have an uncanny resemblance to "straw men." Third, I have suggested changes that might alleviate some of the weaknesses. Finally, I have organized the following discussion into a series of critical questions.

What is a Reward?

This may seem like an odd problem to some. We defined a reward in Chapter 1 as a positively valued activity or object. It was something that met a person's need or reduced a drive. Unfortunately, difficulties arise when we attempt to find actual examples of rewards.

Sometimes an object or activity that is typically considered a reward can be a cost under certain circumstances. For example, we might consider another's assistance to be a reward. If we are performing a tedious task, another's help might be most valued. However, there are times when another's assistance may be costly. This author has noted that when moving into a new neighborhood, one's new neighbors will often offer or impose their help. As noted by Blau (1964a), the acceptance of a reward entails an obligation to repay the reward. As the obligation is repaid another exchange may take place, and suddenly an unanticipated exchange relationship has developed. Consequently, the neighbors' assistance may require that one invite the neighbor over for supper at some future time. The neighbor may feel obligated to invite the new person over for a meal and so on. Therefore, the initial assistance has costs associated with it in terms of obligations.

In addition, people may not find social approval rewarding in certain circumstances. For example, a compliment from an unappealing person is no reward. During the recent (1980) presidential election, Ronald Reagan was endorsed by the Ku Klux Klan, but quickly announced that he did not want their endorsement. Research by Novak and Lerner (1968) demonstrated that perceiving oneself as highly similar in attitudes to a person who was described as emotionally unstable led to a greater desire to avoid that person than if the person was perceived as highly similar and emotionally stable. Thus, consensual validation for one's attitudes from a person with undesirable characteristics prompts avoidance responses rather than approach.

In addition to the ambiguity between reward and costs, we have difficulty determining the value of rewards. Homans (1961, 1974) argues that the value of a reward is determined by the quantity of that resource one has received in the recent past. The more one has received, the less valuable any further unit of that resource becomes. However, we often find it difficult to determine how much and how frequently one has received of a given resource. One must either follow (or have someone follow) the person around and record the frequency of receiving a resource or ask the person about how much the resource is valued. While the first response is fairly easy to do for animals in an experiment (e.g., record how often the animal has been fed), it is very difficult for humans. The second response may be subject to distortion. People may not be willing or able to describe to us the value they place on various objects or activities.

Consequently, a person may have to test a variety of resources to see which ones produce the desired response. It is this process that has led to the most frequent criticism of Homans' Operant Psychology Approach. Scholars often suggest that Homans' approach is a tautology (see Chadwick-Jones, 1976, and Emerson, 1976 for the most recent discussion of this debate). In other words, Homans' "success proposition" and "value proposition" constitute definitions rather than propositions. A reward is anything that causes some response to be repeated after the reward is given. An object or activity has value to the extent that it is able to cause a response to be repeated after it is administered. This criticism does not imply that the reward and the response are the same entity, as would be the case with a logical tautology (Liska, 1969). The reward and the response can be measured separately. The problem is that an object cannot be determined to be rewarding until after it is administered.

To some, this criticism may seem like typical academic concern over matters of little importance. However, the charge of tautology is important to both social scientists and practitioners of communication. For social scientists, a relational tautology may mean that the theory and subsequent hypotheses may not be falsifiable. A theory that cannot be disproved is of no value. While some support has been found for Homans' propositions (e.g., Crosbie, 1972), let us say that a study was done in which social approval was provided in exchange for compliance but no compliance was forthcoming in a later similar situation. Assuming no design problems in the study, one is faced with the difficulty of explaining the results. Do the results mean that social approval is not a reinforcer in this situation or do they imply that Homans' theory is false? If the propositions of Homans' theory are tautological, then we do not know which of the two interpretations is correct.

For the practitioner of interpersonal communication, the tautology may seem like a very real part of life. In communicating with another, we try a variety of strategies until we find the one that works (i.e., provides us with the response we desired). People actually involved in communication probably determine what is rewarding to another in the same tautological fashion as social scientists.

One way to resolve this problem is to focus on creating lists of resources in advance of their use. Of particular utility would be generalized reinforcers (i.e., resources most people judge to be valuable). Foa and Foa (1974, 1976) have made great strides toward a description of these rewards. However, even their focus on resources is still ambiguous; for instance, it is uncertain into which category self-disclosure might fall. Indeed, they argue that such ambiguity is an important area of study in interpersonal communication.

Liska (1969) has suggested that relational tautologies can be evaluated and are useful under some circumstances. We may use Homans' theory as a mechanism for cataloguing objects and activities that are rewarding and the conditions under which their value seems to increase. In essence, our knowledge increases even though the validity of the theory cannot be tested.

A related problem concerns the rate of exchange for the rewards. Since value is difficult to determine, identifying the relative value of objects and activities is also difficult. We noted in Chapter 1 that people often have difficulty describing how much one social reward is worth in relation to another.

Finally we must determine if communication is indeed a reward (or cost) and if it can serve as a reinforcer. Certainly some measurement techniques have been developed that will allow us to measure the exchanges of rewards in a conversation (e.g., see Longabaugh, 1963), but can communication be equated with a reinforcement as described by operant psychology? Some experimental psychologists might shudder at the "liberal" interpretation we have made of reinforcement in this text.

Individuals who wish to employ the Social Exchange Theories will need to address the issue of "What is a reward?" It is an issue which has not come close to resolution in the last two decades of debate. However, it should be noted that this controversy has not hampered empirical research using the Social Exchange Theories (e.g., Weinstein, Devaughan, and Wiley, 1969; Worthy, Gray and Kahn, 1969; Crosbie, 1972).

What is Fair?

Assuming that we can specify what a reward is, the next issue is understanding what constitutes a "fair exchange" of resources. As we have noted previously, the Social Exchange Theories assume that a fair exchange is one that is consistent with distributive justice or is judged to be equitable. One's profits divided by investments should be equal to another's profits divided by investments. Yet others have argued that there are multiple ways to exchange resources in a fair manner (see Cook, 1975; Cook and Parcel, 1977). Meeker (1971) has argued that an individual decision maker may choose to exchange resources according to a number of exchange rules including rationality (i.e., maximize joint profits), altruism (i.e., maximize other's profits), group-gain (i.e., maximize the difference between own and another's profits), status consistency (i.e., try to keep the difference between own and other's profits the same) or reciprocity (i.e., base one's exchanges on what the other has done for self in the past). This model also assumes that a person will use that exchange rule that imposes little or no personal cost. Even though the person's exchanges may be guided by an altruistic exchange rule, as soon as the costs become too great, the person will switch rules.

Leventhal (1976), Lerner (1974, 1975, 1977) and Ridley and Avery (1979) have provided more complete descriptions of alternative methods of resource distribution. Leventhal (1976) has argued that the distribution rules may be of three forms. First, resources may be distributed based upon a person's contributions. The "contribution rule" assumes outcomes will match contributions. Second, resources may be distributed based upon a person's legitimate needs for a resource. The "needs rule" assumes that the person should receive sufficient resources so that legitimate needs are fulfilled and suffering avoided. Finally, resources may be distributed based upon equality. The "equality rule" assumes that both relational partners should divide rewards equally, regardless of their legitimate needs or contributions.

Leventhal believes that people go through a sequence of steps when deciding how resources should be distributed. First, an individual decides which rules are most applicable in this situation. This implies that people weigh the three rules differentially according to their importance. The more importance, the greater the weight attached to that rule. A variety of factors may influence the weights. In general, a person applies different weights based upon the impact of the rule on own self-interest, perceptions of whether other people would view this rule as appropriate, and the availability of accurate information about the situation. In addition, a person also is influenced by specific factors that influence each of the rules individually. Leventhal suggests that the "contribution rule" will receive greater weight whenever the situation is one in which the quality of a person's performance is imperative. Certainly, work situations are an example where resources are distributed based upon competence. The importance of the "needs rule" is hypothesized to be affected by liking for the relational partner, recent success or failure by the perceiver, and the amount of resource needed to satisfy the other's need. The more one likes the relational partner, has experienced recent success, and perceives the demands as relatively small, the more weight the person will attach to the "needs rule." Finally, Leventhal argues that the "equality rule" will receive greater weight whenever the individual is seeking to avoid conflict and is cognitively complex.

Based upon the weightings, the second step involves estimating how much a person deserves based upon one or more of the distribution rules. For example, a person might compare the amount of resources that will be given based upon the "needs rule" with the "equality rule." This process is thought to occur often with little self-awareness. In other words, the perceiver may not be consciously comparing all the factors.

Third, the person combines all the previous information and determines the final amount and types of resources deserved by another. Finally, an evaluation of the outcomes is made after the final decision. Does the distribution of resources appear to be fair after all?

Lerner's (1974, 1975, 1977) model focuses on the "personal contract" as a key determinant for distributing resources. Children and presumably unsocialized adults operate on a "pleasure principle." They tend to engage in whatever behavior provides immediate gratification, regardless of the cost to others. As the child matures, reality impinges. The child develops a "personal contract." Lerner (1974: 332) writes, "he develops a *personal contract* with himself to give up the directly obtainable gratifications and to undertake certain efforts and suffer self-deprivation on the assumption that these behaviors will be followed by more desired outcomes." The person comes to believe that sacrifice will result in later benefits. Consequently, a person deserves certain benefits based on previous behavior.

With the recognition that benefits also depend upon other people, the child will learn to control desires for selfish gain and become concerned for what others deserve. Thus, the individual becomes a long term thinker. If I sacrifice my own outcomes, I deserve to receive benefits at some time in the future. To the extent that I violate the "personal contracts" of others by being exploitative, I increase the probability that I will not get the benefits I deserve.

Like Leventhal, Lerner suggests that a variety of exchange rules or "forms of justice" will be used that are consistent with the "personal contract." These forms of justice are explained in conjunction with the types of relationships in which they will most likely be used. The first type is called an "identity relationship." In this case, two people feel empathy for each other as individuals or for the role played by each other. For example, a married couple may form an interpersonal relationship where they know each other so well that their interests become highly intertwined. They believe what is good for one is good for the other. In such relationships, Lerner suggests that resources are distributed based upon need. This form of justice is similar to what Lerner has called "Marxist Justice" in which rewards are distributed based upon the greatest need. If a married couple has a relatively noninterpersonal relationship where the partners relate primarily on the sociological roles of husband and wife, then resources will be distributed based upon social obligations or contracts. The husband provides resources to his wife based upon what he thinks he would want if he occupied the role of wife. The husband is empathic, not with the wife as an individual but with the role.

Unit relationships do not involve a fusion of self and other. They simply imply that the two people see each other as being similar in some respect. The relational partners may be working toward some mutual goal or share common attributes. When two people perceive themselves as having similar characteristics or abilities, then "parity justice" may guide the distribution of resources. The partners perceive they should receive equal resources regardless of contributions. If the unit relationships implies that the two people see each other as occupying similar roles (e.g., same authority level of an organization), then the partners believe that the resources should be distributed on the bases of equity. One should receive resources based upon contribution or investment.

Nonunit relationships are those in which two partners see each other as being in conflict. Certainly, Scanzoni's (1972) model suggests that husbands and wives find themselves in nonunit relationships quite often. When the two individuals see themselves as being in conflict, the distribution of resources is based upon "Darwinian Justice." This form of justice implies that the two relational partners will attempt to establish dominance over each other. "Survival of the fittest" becomes the method of resource distribution. If the conflict is between people who are occupants of roles, then the form of resource distribution is competitive. The person with the greater abilities or authority receives the greater amount of resources.

While Leventhal and Lerner have focused on how individuals decide which exchange rule to implement, Ridley and Avery (1979) have focused on how one's social network of significant others influence exchange patterns. Based on the work of Burns and his associates (1971, 1972, 1973) and Sahlins (1965, 1968), Ridley and Avery have identified five types of exchange patterns. First, two people may develop a mutually exploitative exchange pattern in which each has a pure self-orientation toward seeking resources and each believes the other is also seeking resources purely out of selfishness. Second, relational partners may develop an exchange pattern characterized by mutual consideration. A person takes into consideration personal self-interest and the self-interest of the relational partner. In addition, both relational partners believe that the other is considering both sets of interests. Third, an exchange pattern focusing on mutual benevolence may develop. In this pattern, one is engaging in behaviors that are in the self-interest of the relational partner rather than in one's own self-interest. Fourth, the parties may be involved in an exchange pattern guided by mutual hostility. In this pattern, both parties are seeking to punish each other. Finally, the pattern may be one described as considerate-benevolent. In such patterns, one party has a positive benevolent orientation toward the other relational party while the other relational party has a self-other orientation. These relationships are characterized by one party taking into consideration the needs of the other party while the other relational party considers both personal needs as well as the needs of the other party. Ridley and Avery have suggested that this form of relationship is common among long-term associations involving power differences. Generally, the party who is taking into consideration both sets of needs has more valuable resources. The benevolent party provides resources to insure that the partner will consider both sets of needs.

Importantly, Ridley and Avery suggest that close relationships typically develop from mutual consideration into mutual benevolence. We move from taking into consideration our own and our partner's self-interest. Relationships that are decaying may move from concern with mutual benevolence to mutual exploitation or mutual hostility.

The exchange pattern is determined by the expectations of one's significant others. Specifically, individuals who have resources the relational partners value, have many types of associations with the relational partners, and are in agreement with significant others about how the relationship should be patterned are most likely to influence the nature of the exchange. We might expect that two relational parties who find that their friends and relatives form a united front of opinion about the relationship may be hard pressed to ignore the demands of their significant others. The significant others might deny valued resources until the two relational parties comply with expectations. This might be the case when a married couple wish to divorce, much to the dismay of family and friends. Family and friends may exert considerable pressure for the couple to remain married.

Ridley and Avery have also hypothesized that most social networks support either conflict exchange patterns (mutual exploitation or hostility) or conflict free patterns (mutual consideration, benevolence, or consideration-benevolence) but not both within a single relationship. Typically, social networks support nonconflict patterns over conflict patterns in close relationships. Thus, the exchange pattern can be forced upon relational partners.

The notions described in the perspectives of Leventhal, Lerner, and Ridley and Avery are critical for interpersonal communication. Too often after presenting exchange principles I have seen students begin analyzing relationships based on considerations of distributive justice. They become concerned when they discover that many relationships, including their own, are based upon some other pattern of exchange than equality or equity. They often come to believe that relationships that are not guided by equity are "bad" relationships. This obviously may not be the case. There may be times when it makes a great deal of sense to distribute resources based upon some other criteria than equity. Certainly a child has minimal investments in a relationship but requires substantial resources to survive. Indeed, Beckman-Brindley and Tavormina (1978) have argued that families may exhibit fluid power relationships in which no one person dominates all of the time. It may be the case within a single relationship that different forms of justice may emerge for different topics. Parity may be the norm for exchanging food resources. Regardless of who bought the food or prepared it, everyone receives equal amounts. Family income may be distributed according to whomever contributed the most to it. Therefore, the person with the greatest income may have the final say in spending patterns. Health and emotional care may be distributed according to "Marxist Justice." The person with the greatest health or emotional need receives the most of that resource.

In addition, we may find that what is considered fair may be determined by the person's involvement in the relationship. An outside observer of a relationship may have a different perspective than the participants. Indeed, people who become involved in another's relationship are often met with statements of "mind your own business!" What may seem inequitable to an observer may not be to a participant.

This point is exemplified by what Gottman et al., (1976) refer to as the "bank account model" of marital interaction. According to this model, spouses attempt to add to the "bank account" by making positive "deposits." Such deposits might include compliments, expressions of love, or assistance. However, a person's communications only constitute a "deposit" if the statements are perceived positively by the receiver of the message. If a source intends communication to be positive and the receiver interprets it in a negative manner then a "communication deficit" is created.

This model has several implications for actors and observers of interpersonal exchange. First, what appears to be a "deposit" by an observer or source of communication may be interpreted as a "withdrawal" by a receiver. Indeed, Gottman et al. (1976) found that married couples characterized as distressed tended to send as many communications that they intended to be positive as did married couples who were not distressed. However, messages meant to be interpreted as positive were more likely to be interpreted as negative in distressed marriages than in nondistressed marriages. Thus, marriages characterized by chronic conflict are more likely to suffer from "communication deficits" than relatively peaceful marriages. An outside observer of the interaction may have great difficulties inferring the responses to a message. I have sometimes heard people remark in disbelief when they hear friends are suffering marital difficulties, "But they were always so nice to each other." The "bank account" model suggests that the interpretation by the receiver is as important as the intent of the source or content of the message.

Second, a person may build up "communication credits." Over the course of a relationship, the partners may have engaged in enough positive communication that they do not have to respond in a reciprocal manner in each communication situation. Research by Gottman et al. (1976) found only minimal support for the notion that positive communication tended to be reciprocated with positive communication to a greater extent in nondistressed than in distressed marriages. Research has also found that friends or spouses are less likely to reciprocate self-disclosure than strangers (Derlega, Wilson, and Chaikin, 1976; Morton, 1978). Thus, an outside observer of a communication sequence may find unreciprocated self-disclosure or compliments to be unfair, while the participants may understand that a "credit" has been built up such that the receiver is not obligated to reciprocate.

Third, a person may provide enough of another resource that communication credit is greater. As noted by Foa and Foa (1974, 1976) one resource may be substituted for a similar resource. Thus, providing sufficient quantities of compliments (increases in status) may build up enough "credit" in love so that the receiver does not have to respond with expressions of love in kind. Thus, an outside observer may have grave difficulties in determining the fairness of an exchange.

Finally, it is necessary that we examine whether violations of fair exchange (however it is defined) are really distressing. Alexander and Simpson (1964) have noted that a victim of a violation of distributive justice may be willing to accept it if norms suggest that the inequity is justified or if the victim can avoid communicating with or thinking about the exploiter. In addition, they doubt that the exploiter always feels distressed at receiving greater rewards than deserved. Indeed, Rivera and Tedeschi (1976) found that exploiters who were being monitored by what they believed was a "lie detector" reported feeling happy with their good fortune. Exploiters filling out questionnaires without the presence of the "lie detector" reported feeling unhappy and guilty about their good fortune. Rivera and Tedeschi interpreted their findings as indicating that exploiters who know their true feelings cannot be determined by others are more likely to communicate false feelings of guilt and unhappiness. This communication is merely a facade to protect their image. They want to appear to be equitable rather than exploitative and avoid the revenge of the victim or supporters.

This interpretation is reinforced by research conducted by Reis and Gruzen (1976). They discovered that subjects tended to adapt their distribution of resources to whomever was monitoring them at the time. If an experimenter monitored their behavior, resources were distributed according to an equity norm, (i.e., those who were most productive received the most rewards). If a person's co-workers were monitoring the person's distribution, then an equality norm prevailed, (i.e., everyone received the same). If, however, no one monitored the distribution, then the person tended to overreward self. Thus, one may violate norms of fairness if one can "get away with it."

Thus, communication scholars need to study the exchange patterns that guide communication. In addition, the conditions that influence the creation of these patterns should be specified.

Are People Really That Self-Interested?

The most frequent criticism I have encountered from students stems from the negative connotations attached to the term "self-interest." Students tend to see self-interest as being related to exploitation. As we noted in Chapter 1, self-interest does not necessarily lead to exploitation. Two people who both are seeking relational rewards will not want to stay in a relationship in which only one benefits. Certainly, the victim will be motivated to restore equity or leave the relationship. The mechanism of self-interest should blunt exploitation, assuming that the two people have available alternative relationships.

Part of the concern about self-interest stems from the belief that altruistic behaviors are different and better. The Social Exchange Theories have a variety of ways to deal with altruism. First, Blau (1964a) admits that altruistic behavior does occur and that it is beyond the scope of his social exchange approach. Rather than deny the existence of altruistic behavior, he simply states he cannot explain it with his theory. This does not imply that altruism is better or worse, it is just different.

Second, some Social Exchange Theories suggest that altruism is disguised self-interest. Homans (1961: 79) wrote: "So long as men's values are altruistic, they can take a profit from altruism too. Some of the greatest profiteers we know are altruists." An altruistic person may find giving resources pleasurable in and of itself. In addition, altruistic people may find that resources are forced upon them anyway. They may not desire the gratitude and prestige associated with altruism but it is often bestowed over their objections.

Finally, some of the exchange perspectives view altruism as being potentially harmful to relationships. Walster, Walster, and Berscheid (1978) argue that altruistic relationships are by definition inequitable relationships. The altruistic person is giving with nothing being provided in return. This often creates power differences in that the recipient of altruistic behaviors may become overly dependent upon the altruist or even be humiliated by the inequity. It may also be potentially exploitative because the giver could be completely drained of resources. Indeed, it is hard to believe that unbridled altruism could be maintained as resources are diminished. Walster, Walster, and Berscheid (1978) suggest that society recognizes these difficulties and put limits on altruism.

Are People Really That Calculating?

While the Social Exchange Theorists point out that their approaches do not assume that people are always calculating their profits or that they are aware that they are calculating them, the description of decision-making certainly implies that people are both active and highly self-aware calculators. I have had many students react to Social Exchange Theory by saying, "Sometimes I think about what I am getting out of a relationship but not often." Their point is a good one. Charles Berger and I (Berger and Roloff, 1980) have argued that most of the theories used in interpersonal communication assume too much cognitive activity and self-awareness. I think several points should be stressed about cognition and social exchange.

First, people may only assess their profits at certain times. Leventhal (1976), for example, has argued that people are only concerned with fairness when they are in a social role that demands that they assess fairness of distribution (e.g., judge or juror), when the person has received complaints that a justice norm is being violated, when a sudden change or event has affected the relationship, and when there is nothing else with which to be concerned. In other words, people may not always be calculating their profits. Calculation occurs when the situation requires it.

Second, people may differ in their inherent tendency to calculate profits. Some individuals may be "active calculators" who are always assessing profits and reacting to inequities. Others may be "passive calculators" and oblivious to profits.

Third, the assessment of profits may not always be accurate. As noted by Heath (1976), people make decisions based upon incomplete and often inaccurate information. In addition, Tversky and Kahneman (1973) have argued that a person's decisions are influenced by the most vivid image or event that has transpired at the time of the decision. I would predict that people who are asked to calculate their profits from a relationship would reach different decisions right after a heated emotional exchange with their relational partners than if their relational partners had just given them a gift.

Fourth, the calculation of profits may be so gradual that people only become aware of it after a certain point in time. Altman and Taylor (1973: 49) have noted, "People do not respond like computers to the social interaction experience; data are not fed into central computer storage areas nor are scores calculated and revised in a mechanical fashion with constant updating of results and immediate revisions of behavior. Thus, reward/cost impacts probably do not register all at once, and behavioral changes are not likely to take place immediately." The gains and losses may be so slight that the person may not realize judgments have been made until they have accumulated to some high level over a long period of time.

Fifth, the calculation of rewards and costs may often occur on a post hoc basis. If Bem's (Bem, 1972) Self-Perception Theory is correct, people may not know what their current profit is until they reflect back about previous behaviors. Indeed, research has indicated that some people who have gone through a divorce spend some time trying to figure out why their relationship went sour (Newman and Langer, 1977; Harvey, Wells, and Alvarez, 1978). They apparently do not forecast future profits. Instead, they try to think back about what happened and may retroactively attribute their relational problems to dismal profits.

Noting whether a person is actively calculating rewards and costs is important because it might lead to differences in behavior. I would argue that people who naturally spend a considerable amount of time assessing rewards and costs or are forced to by the situation differ from those who do not in four ways. First, the "active calculator" is more likely to become aware of inequities in relationships. Because the relationship is under constant scrutiny, the probability of discovering inequity should increase. Indeed, the person who ignores such calculation may overlook a number of relational problems. They are people who after having an inequity pointed out say, "I never really thought about it before." Second, the "active calculator" may engage in greater behavior variability than those who are less active. Because of their greater awareness of inequities, the constant calculator may be adjusting behavior more often. Third, the "active calculator" may delay responses whereas the "passive calculator" may respond quickly with habitual or unplanned behavior. The process of assessing profits takes time. Indeed, I have heard some people in the business community complain about academicians because they take too long to reach a decision and then the decision is filled with "maybes." People who assess profits to greater degrees should be particularly cautious. Fourth, the "active calculator" may suffer energy drain. Thinking takes time and effort. Keeping all the rewards and costs of every relationship in line should be particularly draining. Consequently, I would predict that even the most "active" calculating is conducted in important relationships and important aspects of those relationships.

Consequently, communication scholars should seek models that will allow consideration of both highly cognitive communication sequences and those that involve less cognition. One such approach was developed by Jones and Gerard (1967). They characterize interpersonal interactions as involving four patterns. The first pattern is called a pseudocontingency. In this communication sequence, each party has a preestablished plan for what they want to say and proceed with the plan without adapting to each other's statements. Such communication situations may arise from highly scripted or ritualistic situations (see Schank and Abelson, 1977). Parties communicate with each other using stereotypes that specify what each party should say. Each party knows what the other is going to say ahead of time and they proceed naturally. Everything is preplanned and determined. Secondly, some communication sequences can be termed reactive contingencies. In such cases, the communication of both parties is completely unplanned. The parties are simply responding to the last thing said by the other person. Jones and Gerard point out that this sequence is not often observed in adults. The third sequence is called asymmetrical contingency. In this pattern, one person's communication is preplanned while the other is determined by the response of the partner. These patterns typically arise when one person has the opportunity to think about what to say in advance of the conversation, whereas the other person has no advance warning. The final pattern is called mutual contingency. In these patterns both parties have plans of action but adapt them to the responses of each other. Two people may plan topics of conversation before a date. However, once the date begins, some of the plans may be abandoned as they adapt to each other.

We might speculate that people who maintain their plans may be engaging in less conscious calculation of alternatives during the interaction.

They have already considered the rewards/costs of their various communication behaviors and stay with them. People who respond in an adaptive fashion, either from lack of opportunity for preplanning or a great deal of natural self-monitoring, may be more conscious of the outcomes of their current behavior as they seek the most rewarding messages.

What About Emotion?

Some react to the exchange perspectives by suggesting that they depersonalize interpersonal relationships because exchange is devoid of emotion. Perhaps their response stems from the notion that economic exchange and business relations are often characterized as impersonal and detached. However, the Social Exchange Theories do address emotion. They certainly suggest that inequity creates anger or distress whereas equity produces happiness. Blau (1964a) suggests that as people continue to exchange with each other, they develop emotional attachments with one another.

In another sense, we may place too much emphasis on emotion in relationships. Scanzoni (1972: 54) writes: "These realities of courtship and marriage tend to be clouded (especially for the never-married) by the romantic love complex, which dictates that prospective partners are not supposed to weigh reward elements, at least consciously. Nonrational, romantic, person-centered considerations are supposed to be paramount—lesser elements too crass to be included. Romantic love thus obscures the premarital bargaining process and places some persons in a situation which may eventually work to their detriment." In other words, people may benefit from a less emotional consideration of their relationships. It may save them from future difficulties.

Can Communication be Described by the Assumptions of Social Exchange?

In the preface of this book I pointed out that communication scholars have engaged in a great deal of academic borrowing. It is also apparent that the Social Exchange Theories have been borrowed from other sources as well. Homans (1961, 1974) has relied heavily upon operant psychology. Blau (1964a) has borrowed from economics. Thibaut and Kelley (1959) have found Activation Theory and Game Theory to be useful starting points. Foa and Foa (1974) work from a variety of psychological theories and Walster, Berscheid, and Walster (1976) have borrowed from the other Social Exchange Theories. Thus, the theories we seek to borrow are indeed borrowed from other sources. Given this situation, it is important that we determine the applicability of the original starting points for communication as well as the theory itself.

Not many scholars have used operant psychology to examine communication processes. Our approaches have tended to be more cognitive. Ekeh (1974) would seem to agree with this state of affairs because he believes that conditioned behavior resulting from operant processes is very different from symbolic behavior associated with communication. Conditioned behavior is characterized as being determined by previous experiences, being static, nonnormative, and not making use of time and space. The person whose behavior is conditioned tends to be limited by what has occurred in the past. Planning for the future or for different situations is not thought to be associated with conditioning. Symbolic behavior is thought to be independent of previous behavior, creative, normative among people in a social system, and making use of time and space. The symbolic person can choose to engage in novel behaviors, and can project ahead and guide behavior accordingly.

While I think Ekeh (1974) would find some of his characterizations of Skinner's Operant Psychology different from Skinner's (Skinner, 1974), I think his analysis is certainly worth considering. If we find that communication behaviors are inherently different than those described by operant psychology, then Homans' approach is of little use. Just as in other disciplines, I doubt that this matter will be easily resolved.

Heath (1976) has noted differences between economic and social exchange that make the use of economic methods difficult in studying communication. In general, our measurement techniques are not sophisticated enough to allow the use of many economic methods. Consequently, Blau's (1964a) model may not be capable of precise predictions.

Thibaut and Kelley (1959) rely upon the methods arising from Game Theory. As noted earlier, they do not attempt to meet the assumptions of Game Theory. In addition, not all social scientists have found experimental games to be acceptable equivalents of actual behaviors (see Chadwick-Jones, 1976: 29-33).

Perhaps the greatest difficulty arising from Foa and Foa's (1974, 1976) Resource Theory is determining exactly which category communication behaviors fit into. We have noted on several occasions the ambiguity involved with categorizing self-disclosure. We need to work with the categories in order to assess how communication may fit into them.

Since Equity Theory builds upon the other Social Exchange Theories, their problems tend to generalize to it. In addition, we need to determine if the alternative exchange rules fit communication patterns better than the ones suggested by Equity Theory.

What Role Does Communication Play in Social Exchange?

Since the Social Exchange Theories were developed outside of communication, we must determine what role it plays in these theories. As noted in Chapter 1, communication might be characterized as a reward in and of itself or as a means to achieving rewards. Either of these conceptualizations require that we readjust our assumptions about communication. If communication is intrinsically rewarding, we need to develop taxonomies which describe the relative value of various types of communication. In addition, we will need to determine the relative value of communication in comparison to other resources.

If communication involves attempts to negotiate the exchange of resources, then scholars need to explore approaches to bargaining and negotiation. Druckman (1977) has provided a way to describe negotiation which may be useful for communication researchers and practitioners. He suggests that negotiation consists of three processes. First, negotiation consists of bargaining. Bargaining involves the exchange of offers and counteroffers as the parties attempt to converge upon some mutually acceptable position. Communication would simply involve transmitting offers of rewards.

For example, we might focus on how a husband and wife bargain over a typical marital problem. Couples often have difficulty meeting the demands of the respective sets of parents for attention. This problem is particularly acute at the holidays, when the parents may wish to maintain traditional gatherings of the entire families. If the spouses live considerable distances from the two sets of parents, it is very difficult to be at both places on the same day. Consequently, the spouses may spend time bargaining over where they will be on the holiday. We might find offers to spend Labor Day with the husband's parents and Thanksgiving with the wife's. We might find that the concession patterns may also be of interest. Who will alter position the most? The husband may revise his initial demands for summer visits with his parents if his wife will agree not to press her demand that her parents be invited to visit in December.

A second process of negotiation is debating. Debating consists of a rhetorical contest between negotiators by which they attempt to convince each other of the validity of their respective offers. From a communication perspective, it would seem important that we determine the rationales the partners provide to each other for why their offers are indeed fair ones. For example, Scanzoni's (1979a) research suggests that some debating tactics used by wives might be characterized as individualistic in that the wife is suggesting that fairness is defined by what is good for her or her husband. Other strategies are more collectivistic, in that they stress the importance of the family for determining fairness.

The final process is termed influencing. Influencing involves the use of coercive tactics. Communication might involve the use of threats or verbal aggression in negotiation.

While these processes are presented as independent of each other, we might find their interaction to be particularly interesting. For example, does the use of influencing tactics increase or decrease the likelihood that our offers will be viewed as fair? Are the rationales for our offers really important for facilitating acceptance? For example, if an offer is extremely discrepant from that of our opponent's, will any rationale lead to its acceptance?

While Druckman's analysis is quite useful in describing open negotiation, we may find that some negotiation in exchange relationships is covert. Strauss (1978: 224-225) has described implicit negotiation: "Some negotiations may be very brief, made without any verbal exchange or obvious gestural manifestation; nevertheless, the parties may be perfectly aware of 'what they are doing'—they may not call this negotiating *bargaining*, but they surely regard its product as some sort of *worked-out* agreement. Other negotiations may be so implicit that the respective parties may not be thoroughly aware that they have engaged in or completed a negotiated transaction. If the latter kind of agreement gets broken by one person, however, the other is sure to experience some feeling, whether surprise, disappointment, annoyance, anger, or even a sense of betrayal or exploitation, but possibly also relief or unexpected pleasure."

Strauss has suggested that implicit negotiation may often be found in family interactions. Certainly, the combination of explicit and implicit negotiation in family interactions may provide an interesting source of inquiry. For example, a husband and wife may spend some time bargaining explicitly and implicitly over holiday gifts. I suspect that statements of "I really don't want anything special this year" may mask other implicit demands. If one has always bought expensive gifts in the past, then the statements of "nothing special" may imply that one had better buy something just as expensive this year. Anything less may create relational difficulties.

In any case, the Social Exchange Theories will require that we explore perspectives which we have not spent considerable time studying in the past.

SUMMARY

I think communication scholars and students should continue and perhaps expand our use of the Social Exchange Theories. The weaknesses associated with the theories are often simply research areas rather than fatal flaws. In most cases, I have suggested methods by which we might deal with them.

These theories have provided us with insights into interpersonal communication. They also do much more than that. In many ways, they integrate communication into a broader range of behaviors we find in interpersonal relationships. They also bring with them fundamental assumptions about human behavior. I urge both students and scholars to recognize their different starting points. I fear that some may be tempted to treat the five approaches as food on a smorgasbord tray, choosing a little of each and disregarding the rest. I think the theories should be treated as separate entities rather than patched together like the Frankenstein monster.

We may also find that the Social Exchange Theories offer an alternative to other approaches taken in interpersonal communication. Communication scholars have chosen to focus on symbolic interaction as a beginning point (e.g., Cushman and Craig, 1976). The Social Exchange Theories provide an alternative and competing approach (see Singlemann, 1972, 1973; Abbott, Brown, and Crosbie, 1973; Mitchell, 1978 for discussions and comparisons of the two perspectives). Communication research could gain from variety and competition.

However, in the final analysis, the worth of the Social Exchange Theories will be determined by the individual students who put their principles into practice and the communication scientists who test hypotheses derived from them.

REFERENCES

ABBOTT, C., C. BROWN, and P. CROSBIE (1973) "Exchange as symbolic interaction: for what?" American Sociological Review 38: 504-506.

ABRAHAMSSON, B. (1970) "Homans on exchange: hedonism revived." American Journal of Sociology 76: 273-285.

ADAMS, J. (1965) "Inequity in social exchange," pp. 267-300 in L. Berkowitz (ed.) Advances in Experimental Social Psychology, Vol. 2. New York: Academic Press.

——— and S. FREEDMAN (1976) "Equity theory revisited: comments and annotated bibliography," pp. 43-90 in L. Berkowitz and E. Walster (eds.) Equity Theory: Toward a General Theory of Social Interaction, Advances in Experimental Social Psychology, Vol. 9. New York: Academic Press.

AJZEN, I. (1977) "Information processing approaches to interpersonal attraction," pp. 51-78 in S. Duck (ed.) Theory and Practice in Interpersonal Attraction. New York: Academic Press.

ALEXANDER, C. and R. SIMPSON (1964) "Balance theory and distributive justice." Sociological Inquiry 34: 182-192.

ALTMAN, I. (1973) "Reciprocity of interpersonal exchange." Journal for Theory of Social Behavior 3: 249-261.

——— and D. TAYLOR (1973) Social Penetration: The Development of Interpersonal Relationships. New York: Holt, Rinehart & Winston.

ARCHER, R. (1979) "Role of personality and the social situation," pp. 28-58 in G. Chelune and Associates (eds.) Self-Disclosure: Origins, Patterns, and Implications of Openness in Interpersonal Relationships. San Francisco: Jossey-Bass.

ARGYLE, M. (1975) Bodily Communication. New York: International Universities Press.

ARONSON, E. and D. LINDER (1965) "Gain and loss of esteem as determinants of interpersonal attractiveness." Journal of Experimental Social Psychology 1: 156-172.

BAHR, S. (1976) "Role competence, role norms and marital control," pp. 179-189 in F. Nye (ed.) Role Structure and Analysis of the Family. Beverly Hills: Sage.

BANDURA, A. (1960) Relationship of Family Patterns to Child Behavior Disorders. Progress Report to United States Public Health Service.

——— (1965) "Influences of models' reinforcement contingencies on the acquisition of imitative responses." Journal of Personality and Social Psychology 1: 589-595.

——— (1971) Social Learning Theory. Morristown, NJ: General Learning Press.

——— (1973) Aggression: A Social Learning Analysis. Englewood Cliffs, NJ: Prentice-Hall.

——— and R. WALTERS (1959) Adolescent Aggression. New York: Ronald Press.

BECKMAN-BRINDLEY, S. and J. TAVORMINA (1978) "Power relationships in families: a social exchange perspective." Family Process 17: 423-436.

BEM, D. (1972) "Self perception theory," pp. 2-62 in L. Berkowitz (ed.) Advances in Experimental Social Psychology, Vol. 6. New York: Academic Press.

BERG, J. and R. ARCHER (1980) "Disclosure or concern: a second look at liking for the norm breaker." Journal of Personality 48: 245-257.

BERGER, C. and R. CALABRESE (1975) "Some explorations in initial interaction and beyond: toward a developmental theory of interpersonal communication." Human Communication Research 1: 99-112.

BERGER, C. and M. ROLOFF (1980) "Social cognition, self-awareness, and interpersonal communication," in B. Dervin and M. Voigt (eds.) Progress in Communication Sciences, Vol. 2. Norwood, NJ: Ablex Publishing.

BERKOWITZ, L. (1969) "Social motivation," pp. 50-135 in G. Lindzey and E. Aronson (eds.) The Handbook of Social Psychology (2nd ed.). Reading, MA: Addison-Wesley.

BERNSTEIN, B. (1975) Class, Codes and Control: Theoretical Studies Toward a Sociology of Language. New York: Schocken.

BERSCHEID, E. and E. WALSTER (1978) Interpersonal Attraction (2nd ed.). Reading, MA: Addison-Wesley.

——— and G. BOHRNSTEDT (1973) "The body image report." Psychology Today 7: 119-131.

BIERSTEDT, R. (1965) "Review of Blau's 'Exchange and Power.'" American Sociological Review 30: 789-790.

BIRCHLER, G., R. WEISS and J. VINCENT (1975) "Multimethod analysis of social reinforcement exchange between maritally distressed and nondistressed spouse and stranger dyads." Journal of Personality and Social Psychology 31: 349-360.

BLAIN, R. (1971a) "Comments on Homans' reply." Sociological Inquiry 41: 24-25.

——— (1971b) "On Homans' psychological reductionism." Sociological Inquiry 41: 3-25.

BLAU, P. (1964a) Exchange and Power in Social Life. New York: John Wiley.

——— (1964b) "Justice in social exchange." Sociological Inquiry 34: 193-206.

——— (1968) "Social exchange," pp. 452-457 in D. Sills (ed.) International Encyclopedia of the Social Sciences, Vol. 7. New York: Macmillan.

BOULDING, K. (1962) "Two critiques of Homans' 'Social Behavior: Its Elementary Forms': an economist's view." American Journal of Sociology 67: 458-461.

BRAIKER, H. and G. KELLEY (1979) "Conflict in the development of close relationships," pp. 135-168 in R. Burgess and T. Huston (eds.) Social Exchange in Developing Relationships. New York: Academic Press.

BREDEMERIER, H. (1978) "Exchange theory," pp. 418-456 in R. Bottomore and R. Nisbet (eds.) A History of Sociological Analysis. New York: Basic Books.

BREHM, J. (1966) A Theory of Psychological Reactance. New York: Academic Press.

BROCK, T. (1968) "Implications of commodity theory for value change," pp. 243-276 in A. Greenwald, T. Brock, and T. Ostrom (eds.) Psychological Foundations of Attitudes. New York: Academic Press.

BURGESS, R. and J. NIELSEN (1977) "Distributive justice and the balance of power," pp. 139-169 in R. Hamblin and J. Kunkel (eds.) Behavioral Theory in Sociology. New Brunswick, NJ: Transaction Books.

BURNS, T. (1972) "A structural theory of value, decision-making, and social interaction." Presented at the Symposium on New Directions in Theoretical Anthropology, Oswego, NY.

——— (1973) "A structural theory of social exchange." Acta Sociologica 16: 183-208.

——— and M. COOPER (1971) Value, Social Power, and Economic Exchange. Stockholm: Samhallsvetareforlaget.

BYRNE, B. (1971) The Attraction Paradigm. New York: Academic Press.

CHADWICK-JONES, J. (1973) "Logical reduction and social psychology." Journal for Theory of Social Behavior 3: 5-21.

——— (1976) Social Exchange Theory: Its Structure and Influence in Social Psychology. New York: Academic Press.

CHAIKIN, A. and V. DERLEGA (1974) "Liking for the norm-breaker in self-disclosure." Journal of Personality 42: 117-129.

——— (1976) "Self-disclosure," pp. 177-209 in J. Thibaut, J. Spence, and R. Carson (eds.) Contemporary Topics in Social Psychology. Morristown, NJ: General Learning Press.

CHRISTIE, R. and F. GEIS (1970) Studies in Machiavellianism. New York: Academic Press.

CLORE, G. (1976) "Interpersonal attraction: an overview," pp. 139-175 in J. Thibaut, J. Spence, and R. Carson (eds.) Contemporary Topics in Social Psychology. Morristown, NJ: General Learning Press.

——— and D. BYRNE (1974) "A reinforcement-affect model of attraction," pp. 143-170 in T. Huston (ed.) Foundations of Interpersonal Attraction. New York: Academic Press.

CLORE, G. and H. MCGUIRE (1974) "Attraction and conversational style." Presented at the Society of Experimental Social Psychology, Urbana, IL.

COHEN, R. (1979) "On the distinction between individual deserving and distributive justice." Journal for Theory of Social Behavior 9: 167-185.

COMSTOCK, G. (1975) Television and Human Behavior: The Key Studies. Santa Monica, CA: Rand.

COOK, K. (1975) "Expectations, evaluations, and equity." American Sociological Review 40: 372-388.

——— and T. PARCELL (1977) "Equity theory: directions for future research." Sociological Inquiry 47: 75-88.

COSER, L. (1956) The Functions of Social Conflict. New York: Macmillan.

COWAN, P. and R. WALTERS (1963) "Studies of reinforcement of aggression: I. Effects of scheduling." Child Development 34: 543-551.

CRAWFORD, L., H. KELLEY, J. PLATZ, and P. FOGEL (1977) "Variations in conflict behavior within close heterosexual relationships." (unpublished)

CROSBIE, P. (1972) "Social exchange and power compliance: a test of Homans' propositions." Sociometry 35: 203-222.

CROWNE, D. and B. STRICKLAND (1961) "The conditioning of verbal behavior as a function of need for social approval." Journal of Abnormal and Social Psychology 63: 395-401.

CUSHMAN, D. and R. CRAIG (1976) "Communication systems: interpersonal implications," pp. 37-58 in G. Miller (ed.) Explorations in Interpersonal Communication. Beverly Hills: Sage.
DAVIS, J. (1962) "Two critiques of Homans' 'Social Behavior: Its Elementary Forms': a sociologist's view." American Journal of Sociology 67: 454-458.
DAY, W. (1975) "Contemporary behaviorism and the concept of intention." Nebraska Symposium on Motivation 28: 65-131.
DERLEGA, V. and J. GRZELAK (1979) "Appropriateness of self-disclosure," pp. 151-176 in G. Chelune and Associates (eds.) Self-Disclosure: Origins, Patterns and Implications of Openness in Interpersonal Relationships. San Francisco: Jossey-Bass.
DERLEGA, V., M. WILSON and A. CHAIKIN (1976) "Friendship and disclosure reciprocity." Journal of Personality and Social Psychology 34: 578-582.
DEUTSCH, M. (1964) "Homans in the Skinner box." Sociological Inquiry 34: 156-165.
——— (1973) The Resolution of Conflict. New Haven, CT: Yale University Press.
——— and R. KRAUSS (1965) Theories in Social Psychology. New York: Basic Books.
DONNENWERTH, G. and U. FOA (1974) "Effect of resource class on retaliation to injustice in interpersonal exchange." Journal of Personality and Social Psychology 29: 785-793.
DRUCKMAN, D. (1977) "Social-psychological approaches to the study of negotiation," pp. 15-44 in D. Druckman (ed.) Negotiations: Social Psychological Perspectives. Beverly Hills: Sage.
DUCK, S. [ed.] (1977) Theory and Practice in Interpersonal Attraction. New York: Academic Press.
EKEH, P. (1974) Social Exchange: The Two Traditions. Cambridge, MA: Harvard University Press.
EKMAN, P., W. FRIESEN, and P. ELLSWORTH (1971) The Face and Emotion. New York: Pergamon.
EMERSON, R. (1969) "Operant psychology and exchange theory," pp. 379-405 in R. Burgess and D. Bushell, Jr. (eds.) Experimental Analysis of Social Processes: Implications for a Behavioral Sociology. New York: Columbia University Press.
——— (1972a) "Exchange theory, part I: a psychological basis for social exchange," Pp. 38-57 in J. Berger, M. Zelditch, Jr., and B. Anderson, (eds.) Sociological Theories in Progress, Vol. 2. Boston: Houghton Mifflin.
——— (1972b) "Exchange theory, part II: exchange relations and network structures," pp. 58-87 in J. Berger, M. Zelditch, Jr., and B. Anderson (eds.) Sociological Theories in Progress, Vol. 2. Boston: Houghton Mifflin.
——— (1976) "Social exchange theory," pp. 335-362 in A. Inkeles, J. Coleman, and N. Smelser (eds.) Annual Review of Sociology, Vol. 2. Palo Alto, CA: Annual Reviews.
FIGES, E. (1970) Patriarchal Attitudes: Women in Society. London: Faber and Faber.
FILLEY, A. (1975) Interpersonal conflict resolution. Glenview, IL: Scott, Foresman.
FOA, E. and U. FOA (1976) "Resource theory of social exchange," pp. 99-131 in J. Thibaut, J. Spence, and R. Carson (eds.) Contemporary Topics in Social Psychology. Morristown, NJ: General Learning Press.

FOA, U. (1971) "Interpersonal and economic resources." Science 171: 345-351.

––– and E. FOA (1972) "Resource exchange: toward a structural theory of interpersonal communication," pp. 291-325 in A. Siegman and B. Pope (eds.) Studies in Dyadic Communication. New York: Pergamon Press.

––– (1974) Societal Structures of the Mind. Springfield, IL: Charles C Thomas.

FROST, J. and W. WILMOT (1978) Interpersonal Conflict. Dubuque, IA: Wm. C. Brown.

GEEN, R. and D. STONNER (1971) "Effects of aggressiveness habit strength on behavior in the presence of aggression-related stimuli." Journal of Personality and Social Psychology 17: 149-153.

GELLES, R. (1972) The Violent Home: A Study of Physical Aggression Between Husbands and Wives. Beverly Hills: Sage.

––– and M. STRAUS (1979) "Determinants of violence in the family: toward a theoretical integration," pp. 549-581 in W. Burr, R. Hill, F. Nye, and I. Reiss (eds.) Contemporary Theories about the Family: Research-Based Theories, Vol. 1. New York: Macmillan.

GERGEN, K. (1969) The Psychology of Behavior Exchange. Reading, MA: Addison-Wesley.

––– (1977) "Social exchange theory in a world of transient fact," pp. 91-114 in R. Hamblin and J. Kunkel (eds.) Behavioral Theory in Sociology. New Brunswick, NJ: Transaction.

GERWIRTZ, J. and D. BAER (1958) "Deprivation and satiation of social reinforcers as drive conditions." Journal of Abnormal and Social Psychology 57: 165-172.

GIBBS, J. (1977) "Homans and the methodology of theory construction," pp. 27-48 in R. Hamblin and J. Kunkel (eds.) Behavioral Theory in Sociology. New Brunswick, NJ: Transaction.

GILBERT, S. and D. HORENSTEIN (1975) "The dyadic effects of self disclosure: level versus valence." Human Communication Research 1: 316-322.

GOTTMAN, J., C. NOTARIUS, H. MARKMAN, S. BANK, B. YOPPI, and M. RUBIN (1976) "Behavior exchange theory and marital decision making." Journal of Personality and Social Psychology 34: 14-23.

GOULDNER, A. (1960) "The norm of reciprocity: a preliminary statement." American Sociological Review 25: 161-178.

GRAY, D. (1971) "Some comments concerning Maris on 'logical adequacy.' " American Sociological Review 36: 706-709.

HARVEY, J., G. WELLS, and M. ALVAREZ (1978) "Attribution in the context of conflict and separation in close relationships," pp. 235-260 in J. Harvey, W. Ickes, and R. Kidd (eds.) New Directions in Attribution Research, Vol. 2. Hillsdale, NJ: Erlbaum Associates.

HEATH, A. (1968a) "Economic theory and sociology: a critique of P. M. Blau's 'Exchange and Power in Social Life.' " Sociology 2: 271-292.

––– (1968b) "MacIntyre on Blau." Sociology 2: 93-96.

––– (1976) Rational Choice and Social Exchange: A Critique of Exchange Theory. Cambridge, England: Cambridge University Press.

HEIDER, F. (1958) The Psychology of Interpersonal Relations. New York: John Wiley.

HILL, C., Z. RUBIN, and L. PEPLAU (1976) "Breakups before marriage: the end of 103 affairs." Journal of Social Issues 32: 147-168.

HOLMES, J. and D. MILLER (1976) "Interpersonal conflict," pp. 265-307 in J. Thibaut, J. Spence, and R. Carson (eds.) Contemporary Topics in Social Psychology. Morristown, NJ: General Learning Press.

HOMANS, G. (1958) "Social behavior as exchange." American Journal of Sociology 63: 597-606.

——— (1961) Social Behavior: Its Elementary Forms. New York: Harcourt Brace Jovanovich.

——— (1967) The Nature of Social Science. New York: Harcourt Brace Jovanovich.

——— (1971a) "Attraction and power," pp. 46-58 in B. Murstein (ed.) Theories of Attraction and Love. New York: Springer-Verlag.

——— (1971b) "Rebuttal to Blain." Sociological Inquiry 41: 25-26.

——— (1971c) "Reply to Blain." Sociological Inquiry 41: 19-24.

——— (1974) Social Behavior: Its Elementary Forms (revised edition). New York: Harcourt Brace Jovanovich.

——— (1976) "Commentary," pp. 231-244 in L. Berkowitz and E. Walster (eds.) Equity Theory: Toward a General Theory of Social Interaction, Advances in Experimental Social Psychology, Vol. 9. New York: Academic Press.

HUESMANN, L. and G. LEVINGER (1976) "Incremental exchange theory: a formal model for progression in dyadic social interaction," pp. 192-230 in L. Berkowitz and E. Walster (eds.) Equity Theory: Toward a General Theory of Social Interaction, Advances in Experimental Social Psychology, Vol. 9. New York: Academic Press.

HUSTON, T. [ed.] (1974) Foundations of Interpersonal Attraction. New York: Academic Press.

JANDT, F. [ed.] (1973) Conflict Resolution Through Communication. New York: Harper & Row.

JOHNSON, W. (1977) "Exchange in perspective; the promises of George C. Homans," pp. 49-90 in R. Hamblin and J. Kunkel (eds.) Behavioral Theory in Sociology. New Brunswick, NJ: Transaction.

JONES, E. and H. GERARD (1967) Foundations of Social Psychology. New York: John Wiley.

KELLEY, H. (1979) Personal Relationships: Their Structures and Processes. Hillsdale, NJ: Erlbaum Associates.

——— and J. THIBAUT (1978) Interpersonal Relations: A Theory of Interdependence. New York: John Wiley.

KELLEY, H., J. CUNNINGHAM, J. GRISHMAN, L. LEFEBVRE, C. SINK, and G. YABLON (1978) "Sex differences in comments made during conflict within close heterosexual pairs." Sex Roles 4: 473-492.

KLEINKE, C. (1979) "Effects of personal evaluations," pp. 59-79 in G. Chelune and Associates (eds.) Self-Disclosure: Origins, Patterns, and Implications of Openness in Interpersonal Relationships. San Francisco: Jossey-Bass.

KNAPP, M. (1978) Social Intercourse: From Greeting to Goodbye. Boston: Allyn & Bacon.

KNUDSON, R., A. SOMMERS, and S. GOLDING (1980) "Interpersonal perception and mode of resolution in marital conflict." Journal of Personality and Social Psychology 38: 751-763.

LAGAIPA, J. (1977) "Interpersonal attraction and social exchange," pp. 129-164 in S. Duck (ed.) Theory and Practice in Interpersonal Attraction. New York: Academic Press.

LANGER, E. (1978) "Rethinking the role of thought in social interaction," pp. 35-58 in J. Harvey, W. Ickes, and R. Kidd (eds.) New Directions in Attribution Research, Vol. 2. Hillsdale, NJ: Erlbaum Associates.

LA ROSSA, R. (1971) Conflict and Power in Marriage: Expecting the First Child. Beverly Hills: Sage.

LEIK, R. and S. LEIK (1977) "Transition to interpersonal commitment," pp. 299-322 in R. Hamblin and J. Kunkel (eds.) Behavioral Theory in Sociology. New Brunswick, NJ: Transaction.

LERNER, M. (1974) "Social psychology of justice and interpersonal attraction," pp. 331-355 in T. Huston (ed.) Foundations of Interpersonal Attraction. New York: Academic Press.

––– (1975) "The justice motive in social behavior: an introduction." Journal of Social Issues 31: 1-19.

––– (1977) "The justice motive: some hypotheses as to its origins and forms." Journal of Personality 45: 1-52.

–––, D. MILLER and J. HOLMES (1976) "Deserving and the emergence of forms of justice," pp. 134-162 in L. Berkowitz and E. Walster (eds.) Equity Theory: Toward a General Theory of Social Interaction, Advances in Experimental Social Psychology, Vol. 9. New York: Academic Press.

LEVENTHAL, G. (1976) "Fairness in social relationships," pp. 211-239 in J. Thibaut, J. Spence, and R. Carson (eds.) Contemporary Topics in Social Psychology. Morristown, NJ: General Learning Press.

LEVINGER, G. (1974) "A three-level approach to attraction: toward an understanding of pair relatedness," pp. 100-120 in T. Huston (ed.) Foundations of Interpersonal Attraction. New York: Academic Press.

––– (1977) "The embrace of lives: changing and unchanging," pp. 1-16 in G. Levinger and H. Raush (eds.) Close Relationships: Perspectives on the Meaning of Intimacy. Amhert: University of Massachusetts Press.

––– (1979) "A social exchange view on the dissolution of pair relationships," pp. 169-196 in R. Burgess and T. Huston (eds.) Social Exchange in Developing Relationships. New York: Academic Press.

––– and J. SNOEK (1972) Attraction in Relationships: A New Look at Interpersonal Attraction. Morristown, NJ: General Learning Press.

LEVI-STRAUSS, C. (1969) The Elementary Structure of Kinship. Boston: Beacon.

LISKA, A. (1969) "Uses and misuses of tautologies in social psychology." Sociometry 32: 444-457.

LOEW, C. (1967) "Acquisition of a hostile attitude and its relationship to aggressive behavior." Journal of Personality and Social Psychology 5: 335-341.

LONGABAUGH, R. (1963) "A category system for coding interpersonal behavior as social exchange." Sociometry 26: 319-343.

LOVAAS, O. (1961) "Effect of exposure to symbolic aggression on aggressive behavior." Child Development 32: 37-44.

LUSTIG, M. and S. KING (1980) "The effect of communication apprehension and situation on communication strategy choice." Human Communication Research 7: 74-82.

MACINTYRE, A. (1967) "A review of P. M. Blau, 'Exchange and Power in Social Life.' " Sociology 1: 199-201.

MACK, R. and R. SNYDER (1957) "The analysis of social conflict—toward an overview and synthesis." Journal of Conflict Resolution 1: 212-248.

MARIS, R. (1970) "The logical adequacy of Homans' social theory." American Sociological Review 35: 1069-1081.

MARIS, R. (1971) "Second thoughts: uses of logic in theory construction." American Sociological Review 36: 713-715.

MARWELL, G. and D. SCHMITT (1967) "Dimensions of compliance-gaining behavior: an empirical analysis." Sociometry 30: 350-364.

MATARAZZO, J., G. SASLOW, A. WIENS, M. WEITMAN, and B. ALLEN (1964) "Interviewer head-nodding and interviewer speech deviations." Psychotherapy 1: 54-63.

McCALL, G. and J. SIMMONS (1978) Identities and Interactions: An Examination of Human Associations in Everyday Life (rev. ed.). New York: Macmillan.

McCALL, M. (1970) "Boundary rules in relationships and encounters," pp. 35-61 in G. McCall, M. McCall, N. Denzin, G. Suttles, and S. Kurth (eds.) Social Relationships. Chicago: AVC.

MEEKER, B. (1971) "Decisions and exchange." American Sociological Review 36: 485-495.

METTEE, D. and E. ARONSON (1974) "Affective reactions to appraisal from others," pp. 236-284 in T. Huston (ed.) Foundations of Interpersonal Attraction. New York: Academic Press.

MILLER, G., F. BOSTER, M. ROLOFF, and D. SEIBOLD (1977) "Compliance-gaining message strategies: a typology and some findings concerning effects of situational differences." Communication Monographs 44: 37-51.

MILLER, G. and H. SIMONS [eds.] (1974) Perspectives on Communication in Social Conflict. Englewood Cliffs, NJ: Prentice-Hall.

MILLER, G. and M. STEINBERG (1975) Between people: A New Analysis of Interpersonal Communication. Palo Alto, CA: Science Research Associates.

MISCHEL, T. (1975) "Psychological explanations and their vicissitudes." Nebraska Symposium on Motivation 28: 133-204.

MITCHELL, J. (1978) Social Exchange, Dramaturgy and Ethnomethodology: Toward a Paradigmatic Synthesis. New York: Elsevier North-Holland.

MORTON, T. (1978) "Intimacy and reciprocity of exchange: comparison of spouses and strangers." Journal of Personality and Social Psychology 36: 72-81.

———, J. ALEXANDER, and I. ALTMAN (1976) "Communication and relationship definition," pp. 105-126 in G. Miller (ed.) Explorations in Interpersonal Communication. Beverly Hills: Sage.

MULKAY, M. (1971) Functionalism Exchange and Theoretical Strategy. London: Routledge and Kegan Paul.

MURSTEIN, B. (1971a) "A theory of marital choice and its applicability to marriage adjustment," pp. 100-151 in B. Murstein (ed.) Theories of Attraction and Love. New York: Springer-Verlag.

——— [ed.] (1971b) Theories of Attraction and Love. New York: Springer-Verlag.

——— (1974) Love, Sex and Marriage Through the Ages. New York: Springer-Verlag.

——— (1976) Who Will Marry Whom? Theories and Research on Marital Choice. New York: Springer-Verlag.

——— (1977) "The stimulus-value-role (SVR) theory of dyadic relationships," pp. 105-128 in S. Duck (ed.) Theory and Practice in Interpersonal Attraction. New York: Academic Press.

NEWMAN, H. and E. LANGER (1977) "Post-divorce adaptation as a function of the attribution of responsibility for the divorce." (unpublished)

NORD, W. (1969) "Social exchange theory: an integrative approach to social conformity." Psychological Bulletin 71: 174-208.

NORTON, R. and L. PETTEGREW (1979) "Attentiveness as a style of communication: a structural analysis." Communication Monographs 46: 13-26.

NOVAK, D. and M. LERNER (1968) "Rejection as a consequence of perceived similarity." Journal of Personality and Social Psychology 9: 147-152.

NYE, F. (1978) "Is choice and exchange theory the key?" Journal of Marriage and the Family 40: 219-233.

——— (1979) "Choice, exchange, and the family," pp. 1-41 in W. Burr, R. Hill, F. Nye, and I. Reiss (eds.) Contemporary Theories about the Family, Vol. II. New York: Macmillan.

——— and S. McLAUGHLIN (1976) "Role competence and marital satisfaction," pp. 191-205 in F. Nye (ed.) Role Structure and Analysis of the Family. Beverly Hills: Sage.

ORVIS, B., H. KELLEY and D. BUTLER (1976) "Attributional conflict in young couples," pp. 353-386 in J. Harvey, W. Ickes, and R. Kidd (eds.) New Directions in Attribution Research, Vol. 1. Hillsdale, NJ: Erlbaum Associates.

PARKE, R., W. EWALL, and R. SLABY (1972) "Hostile and helpful verbalizations as regulators of nonverbal aggression." Journal of Personality and Social Psychology 23: 243-248.

PARKE, R., C. WIEDERHOLT, and R. SLABY (1972) "The effect of exposure to a model's aggressive verbalizations on the observer's motor aggression." (unpublished)

PATTERSON, G., M. LUDWIG, and B. SONODA (1961) "Reinforcement of aggression in children." (unpublished)

PATTERSON, G. and J. REID (1970) "Reciprocity and coercion: two facets of social systems," pp. 133-177 in C. Neuringer and J. Michael (eds.) Behavior Modification in Clinical Psychology. Englewood Cliffs, NJ: Prentice-Hall.

PEPLAU, L. (1977) "Power in dating couples." (unpublished)

PRICE, R. (1971) "On Maris and the logic of time." American Sociological Review 36: 711-713.

RAUSCH, H., W. BARRY, R. HERTEL, and M. SWAIN (1974) Communication, Conflict and Marriage. San Francisco: Jossey-Bass.

REIS, H. and J. GRUZEN (1976) "On mediating equity, equality, and self-interest: the role of self-preservation in social exchange." Journal of Experimental Social Psychology 12: 487-503.

RIDLEY, C. and A. AVERY (1979) "Social network influence on the dyadic relationship," pp. 223-246 in R. Burgess and T. Huston (eds.) Social Exchange in Developing Relationships. New York: Academic Press.

RIVERA, A. and H. TEDESCHI (1976) "Public versus private reactions to positive inequity." Journal of Personality and Social Psychology 34: 895-900.

ROLOFF, M. (1976) "Communication strategies, relationships, and relational changes," pp. 173-196 in G. Miller (ed.) Explorations in Interpersonal Communication. Beverly Hills: Sage.

——— (1978) "The influence of sex, nature of relationships with another and modes of conflict resolution on conflict resolution communication." Presented at the Speech Communication Association Convention, Minneapolis.

——— (1980) "The impact of differential socialization on the use of pro- and anti-social modes of conflict resolution by males and females." Presented at the International Communication Association Convention, Acapulco, Mexico.

——— (1981) "Individual differences in communication: where are they?" Presented at the International Communication Association Convention, Minneapolis.

——— (forthcoming) "Interpersonal and mass communication scripts: an interdisciplinary link," in G. C. Wilhoit (ed.) Mass Communication Review Yearbook, Vol. 2. Beverly Hills: Sage.

——— and E. BARNICOTT (1978) "The situational use of pro- and antisocial compliance-gaining strategies by high and low Machiavellians," pp. 193-208 in B. Rubin (ed.) Communication Yearbook II. New Brunswick, NJ: Transaction.

——— (1979) "The influence of dogmatism on the situational use of pro- and anti-social compliance-gaining strategies." Southern Speech Communication Journal 45: 37-54.

ROLOFF, M. and B. GREENBERG (1979a) "Resolving conflict: methods used by TV characters and teenage viewers." Journal of Broadcasting 23: 285-295.

——— (1979b) "Sex difference in choice of modes of conflict resolution in real-life and television." Communication Quarterly 27: 3-12.

——— (1980) "TV, peer, and parent models for pro- and anti-social conflict behaviors." Human Communication Research 6: 340-351.

ROLOFF, M. and J. REINER (1978) "Social exchange theory: its impact on interpersonal communication." Presented at Southern Speech Communication Association Convention, Atlanta.

ROSEKRANS, M. and W. HARTUP (1967) "Imitative influences of consistent and inconsistent response consequences to a model on aggressive behavior in children." Journal of Personality and Social Psychology 7: 429-434.

ROSS, M. and F. SICOLY (1978) "Egocentric biases in recall and attribution." (unpublished)

RUBIN, J. and B. BROWN (1975) The Social Psychology of Bargaining and Negotiation. New York: Academic Press.

RUBIN, Z. (1973) Liking and Loving: An Invitation to Social Psychology. New York: Holt, Rinehart & Winston.

SAHLINS, M. (1965) "On the sociology of primitive exchange," pp. 139-236 in M. Banton (ed.) The Relevance of Models for Social Anthropology. New York: Praeger.

——— (1968) Tribesmen. Englewood Cliffs, NJ: Prentice-Hall.

SCANZONI, J. (1970) Opportunity and the Family. New York: Macmillan.

——— (1972) Sexual Bargaining: Power Politics in the American Marriage. Englewood Cliffs, NJ: Prentice-Hall.

——— (1979a) Sex Roles, Women's Work, and Marital Conflict. Lexington, MA: D. C. Heath.

——— (1979b) "Social processes and power in families," pp. 295-316 in W. Burr, R. Hill, F. Nye, and I. Reiss (eds.) Contemporary Theories about the Family: Research-Based Theories, Vol. 1. New York: Macmillan.

SCHANK, R. and R. ABELSON (1977) Scripts, Plans, Goals and Understanding: An Inquiry into Human Knowledge Structures. Hillsdale, NJ: Erlbaum Associates.

SCHEFLIN, A. (1972) Body Language and Social Order: Communication as Behavior Control. Englewood Cliffs, NJ: Prentice-Hall.

SCOTT, M. and W. POWERS (1978) Interpersonal Communication: A Question of Needs. Boston: Houghton Mifflin.

SECORD, P. and C. BACKMAN (1974) Social Psychology (2nd ed.). New York: McGraw-Hill.

SILLARS, A. (1980) "Stranger and spouse as target persons for compliance-gaining strategies." Human Communication Research 6: 265-279.

SIMPSON, R. (1972) Theories of Social Exchange. Morristown, NJ: General Learning Press.

SINGLEMANN, P. (1972) "Exchange as symbolic interaction: convergences between two theoretical perspectives." American Sociological Review 37: 414-424.

——— (1973) "On reification of paradigms: reply to Abbott, Brown, and Crosbie." American Sociological Review 37: 507-509.

SKIDMORE, W. (1975) Sociology's Models of Man: The Relationships of Models of Men to Sociological Explanation in Three Sociological Theories. New York: Gordon & Breach.

——— (1979) Theoretical Thinking in Sociology (2nd ed.) Cambridge, England: Cambridge University Press.

SKINNER, B. F. (1974) About Behaviorism. New York: Knopf.

SNYDER, M. (1974) "The self-monitoring of expressive behavior." Journal of Personality and Social Psychology 30: 526-537.

——— (1979) "Self-monitoring processes," pp. 86-131 in L. Berkowitz (ed.) Advances in Experimental Social Psychology, Vol. 12. New York: Academic Press.

STEINFATT, T. and G. MILLER (1974) "Communication in game theoretic models of conflict," pp. 14-75 in G. Miller and H. Simons (eds.) Perspectives on Communication in Social Conflict. Englewood Cliffs, NJ: Prentice-Hall.

STEINMETZ, S. (1979) "Disciplinary techniques and their relationship to aggressiveness, dependency, and conscience," pp. 405-438 in W. Burr, R. Hill, F. Nye, and I. Reiss (eds.) Contemporary Theories About the Family: Research-Based Theories, Vol. 1. New York: Macmillan.

STERNBERG, D. and E. BEIER (1977) "Changing patterns of conflict." Journal of Communication 27: 97-99.

STRAUSS, A. (1978) Negotiations. San Francisco: Jossey-Bass.

STRAYHORN, J. (1978) "Social-exchange theory: cognitive restructuring in marital therapy." Family Process 17: 437-448.

STUART, R. (1969) "Operant interpersonal treatment for marital discord." Journal of Consulting and Clinical Psychology 33: 675-682.

SWENSEN, C. (1973) Introduction to Interpersonal Relations. Glenview, IL: Scott, Foresman.

TAYLOR, D. (1979) "Motivational bases," pp. 110-150 in G. Chelune and Associates (eds.) Self-Disclosure: Origins, Patterns and Implications of Openness in Interpersonal Relationships. San Francisco: Jossey-Bass.

——— and I. ALTMAN (1975) "Self-disclosure as a function of reward-cost outcomes." Sociometry 38: 18-31.

TEDESCHI, J. and T. BONOMA (1977) "Measures of last resort: coercion and aggression in bargaining," pp. 213-242 in D. Druckman (ed.) Negotiations: Social Psychological Perspectives. Beverly Hills: Sage.

––– and B. SCHLENKER (1972) "Influence, decision, and compliance," pp. 346-418 in J. Tedeschi (ed.) The Social Influence Processes. Chicago: AVC.

TEDESCHI, J. and P. ROSENFELD (1980) "Communication in bargaining and negotiation," pp. 225-248 in M. Roloff and G. Miller (eds.) Persuasion: New Directions in Theory and Research. Beverly Hills: Sage.

TEDESCHI, J., B. SCHLENKER, and T. BONOMA (1973) Conflict, Power and Games: The Experimental Study of Interpersonal Relations. Chicago: AVC.

TEDESCHI, J., B. SCHLENKER, and S. LINDSKOLD (1972) "The exercise of power and influence: the source of influence," pp. 287-345 in J. Tedeschi (ed.) The Social Influence Processes. Chicago: AVC.

THELEN, M. and W. SOLTZ (1969) "The effect of vicarious reinforcement on imitation in two social racial groups." Child Development 40: 879-887.

THIBAUT, J. and H. KELLEY (1959) The Social Psychology of Groups. New York: John Wiley.

TURK, H. and R. SIMPSON (1971) Institutions and Social Exchange: The Sociologies of Talcott Parsons and George C. Homans, Indianapolis: Bobbs-Merrill.

TURNER, J. (1974) The Structure of Sociological Theory. Homewood, IL: Irwin.

TURNER, R. (1961) "Review of social behavior: its elementary forms." American Sociological Review 26: 635-636.

TURNER, S. (1971) "The logical adequacy of the 'logical adequacy of Homans' social theory.'" American Sociological Review 36: 709-711.

TVERSKY, A. and D. KAHNEMAN (1974) "Judgment under uncertainty: heuristics and biases." Science 185: 1124-1131.

VERPLANCK, W. (1955) "The control of the content of conversation: reinforcement of statements of opinion." Journal of Abnormal and Social Psychology 51: 668-676.

WALLER, W. and R. HILL (1951) The Family: A Dynamic Interpretation. New York: Dryden Press.

WALSTER, E., E. BERSCHEID, and G. WALSTER (1976) "New directions in equity research," pp. 1-42 in L. Berkowitz and E. Walster (eds.) Equity Theory: Toward a General Theory of Social Interaction, Advances in Experimental Social Psychology, Vol. 9. New York: Academic Press.

WALSTER, E., G. WALSTER, and E. BERSCHEID (1978) Equity: Theory and Research. Boston: Allyn & Bacon.

WALSTER, E., G. WALSTER, and S. TRAUPMANN (1977) "Equity and premarital sex." (unpublished)

WALTERS, R. and M. BROWN (1963) "Studies of reinforcement of aggression: III. Transfer of responses to an interpersonal situation." Child Development 34: 563-571.

WALTERS, R., R. PARKE, and V. CANE (1965) "Timing of punishment and the observation of consequences to others as determinants of response inhibition." Journal of Experimental Child Psychology 2: 10-30.

WATZLAWICK, P., J. BEAVIN, and D. JACKSON (1967) Pragmatics of Human Communication: A Study of Interactional Patterns, Pathologies, and Paradoxes. New York: Norton.

WEINSTEIN, E., W. DEVAUGHAN, and M. WILEY (1969) "Obligations and the flow of deference in exchange." Sociometry 32: 1-12.

WEISS, R. (1975) "Contracts, cognition, and change: a behavioral approach to marriage therapy." Consulting Psychology 5: 15-26.

——— (1976) "The emotional impact of marital separation." Journal of Social Issues 32: 135-145.

WILMOT, W. (1979) Dyadic Communication (2nd ed.). Reading, MA: Addison-Wesley.

WORTHY, M., A. GRAY, and G. KAHN (1969) "Self-disclosure as an exchange process." Journal of Personality and Social Psychology 13: 59-63.

ABOUT THE AUTHOR

MICHAEL E. ROLOFF is Assistant Professor of Communication Studies at Northwestern University. He received his Ph.D. in communication from Michigan State University and was Assistant Professor of Human Communication at the University of Kentucky prior to moving to Northwestern. His interests include persuasion, bargaining and negotiation, and interpersonal conflict resolution. He recently coedited *Persuasion: New Directions in Theory and Research* with Dr. Gerald R. Miller.